Easy Cast Iron Skillet Recipes: The Best Iron Skillet Meals Cookbook

OLIVIA NELSON

Introduction

I have a love affair with cooking in my cast iron skillet. Not only are they incredibly durable and versatile, iron skillets also make a beautiful way to present food with their rustic charm.

As much as I love my cast iron, I know how difficult it can be to come up with new meal ideas the family won't get bored with. That's why I have put together this book of 150 awesome recipes that you can cook in your skillet. Not only are these recipes incredibly easy to make, they are also amazingly delicious!

I hope you enjoy these recipes as much as my family and I do!

Before you begin (or continue) to use your cast iron skillet, there are a few things that I will go over first.

Cast Iron Skillet Cleaning

Do not put your cast iron skillet in the dishwasher. This will remove the seasoning on the pan and it will rust.

Do not clean your skillet with soap as this will also strip

the pan of its seasoning.

Do not use metal scrub pads. These can scratch and damage your pan.

Clean your skillet with coarse salt and hot water. You can also boil some water with salt on the stove to remove "stuck-on" food particles. Wait until it cools off and then use a plastic brush or sponge with water to remove the food debris.

How to Remove Rust

In the event that you accidentally put your cast iron skillet in the dishwasher or it develops some rust on it, no need to worry. Reseason the pan (see directions for reseasoning).

Seasoning a Cast Iron Skillet

Cover the bottom oven rack with aluminum foil.

Preheat your oven to 250 degrees.

Wipe the pan clean.

Coat the **entire pan** (inside, outside, bottom, sides, handle) with a thin layer of: Crisco, olive oil, lard, coconut oil, vegetable oil, canola oil, or other oil or fat you have on hand.

Bake on rack above foil for 15 minutes.

Remove from oven and allow pan to cool before storing.

Reseasoning a Cast Iron Skillet

Cover the bottom oven rack with aluminum foil.

Preheat your oven to 350 degrees.

Remove rust with a wet sponge or plastic scrub brush.

Coat the **entire pan** (inside, outside, bottom, sides, handle) with a thin layer of: Crisco, olive oil, lard, coconut oil, vegetable oil, canola oil, or other oil or fat you have on hand. Whatever oil or fat you use should have a smoke point higher than 350 degrees.

Place pan upside down on rack above foil for one hour.

Turn oven off and let pan cool in the oven.

Recipes

Breakfast

Potato and Sausage Frittata

Ingredients

1 (16 ounce) carton liquid eggs

2 cups hash browns, shredded

1 pound of breakfast sausage

3 cups fresh spinach

½ cup mozzarella cheese, shredded

½ cup red onion, diced

4 tablespoons olive oil

salt and pepper

Preparation

Preheat oven to 400 degrees.

Add sausage to skillet and cook over medium heat. Once sausage is browned, remove from pan and set aside.

Place 1 tablespoon of olive oil in skillet over medium heat. Add hash browns and season liberally with salt and pepper. Stir occasionally and cook for about 4 minutes. Remove hash browns from pan and set aside.

Place 1 tablespoon of olive oil in skillet and add onions and spinach. Sauté for about 3 minutes and remove from pan.

Add last 2 tablespoons of olive oil to skillet and place potatoes back in pan, spreading evenly. Next layer the sausage, then vegetables, eggs, and cover the top with cheese. Season with salt and pepper.

Bake in oven for 15 minutes.

Blueberry Pancake Skillet

Ingredients

1½ cups all-purpose flour

1¼ cup fresh blueberries

1 cup + 2 tablespoon milk

2 eggs, room temperature

4 tablespoons sugar + 1 teaspoon sugar for topping

3 tablespoons butter, melted + 1 tablespoon for skillet

2 teaspoons baking powder

½ teaspoon ground cinnamon

1 tablespoon orange zest

Garnishes: powdered sugar and maple syrup

Preparation

Place skillet in oven and preheat to 375 degrees.

In a bowl, whisk flour, 4 tablespoons of sugar, baking powder, cinnamon and orange zest together.

In a microwave-safe bowl, melt 3 tablespoons of butter. Whisk in milk first and then add the eggs and whisk to combine.

Combine milk mixture with flour mixture and whisk together just until it starts to come together.

Remove skillet from oven and carefully coat with the remaining tablespoon of butter.

Pour pancake batter into skillet and spread evenly.

Drop blueberries evenly onto batter.

Place skillet back in oven and bake for approximately 25 minutes, or until done.

Remove from oven and let rest 5 minutes.

Lightly dust pancake with powdered sugar and serve with maple syrup.

Kielbasa and Potato Hash

Ingredients

1 pound potatoes, thinly sliced into bite-sized pieces

14 ounces of turkey kielbasa, cut into ¼" rounds

2 bell peppers, chopped

1 onion, thinly sliced

3 tablespoons extra-virgin olive oil

1 tablespoon unsalted butter

salt and pepper to taste

Preparation

Over medium-high heat, add 2 tablespoons of olive oil and butter to skillet.

When butter is melted, place potatoes in pan and add salt and pepper.

Cook without stirring, about 7 minutes or until potatoes are brown on bottom. Turn potatoes over and cook for another 5 minutes (without stirring) to brown the other side. Remove potatoes from skillet and set aside.

Add remaining 1 tablespoon of olive oil to pan. Add kielbasa and cook for about 3 minutes, stirring occasionally and browning on both sides.

Add onions and peppers to kielbasa and cook until tender, about 5 minutes. Salt and pepper to taste.

Place potatoes back in pan and stir together. Cook for about 2 minutes and remove from heat.

Vegetable, Bacon & Egg Skillet

Ingredients

4-6 bacon strips, cooked and roughly chopped

1 (12 ounce) can evaporated milk

1½ cups shredded potatoes, (I prefer frozen)

1 cup shredded smoked cheddar cheese

1 cup zucchini, diced or finely sliced

4 eggs

¾ cup peas, fresh or frozen

¾ cup carrots, finely sliced or shredded

¼ cup green onions, chopped

2 garlic cloves, minced

1 teaspoon chopped fresh thyme

salt and pepper

Crisco or oil (for seasoning pan)

Preparation

Preheat oven to 350 degrees.

Grease your cast iron skillet with Crisco or oil.

In a bowl, mix together potatoes, bacon, peas, carrots, zucchini, green onions, garlic and 1/2 cup cheese.

Place mixture in skillet, spreading evenly.

In a bowl, beat eggs and whisk in evaporated milk. Add salt and pepper.

Pour egg mixture over potatoes and top with remaining cheese.

Bake for 50 minutes, until top is golden brown.

Let rest 5 minutes before serving.

Breakfast Skillet

Ingredients

6 cups hash browns or diced potatoes, (I use frozen)

6 bacon slices

1 cup sharp cheddar cheese

6 eggs

1 onion

salt and pepper

butter

Preparation

Cook bacon in your skillet and drain on paper towel.

Add onion and cook for 3 minutes, until tender.

Add potatoes and salt & pepper to taste. Spread potatoes evenly in pan and cook without stirring so they brown on bottom. Once they are a nice golden brown (about 7 minutes), flip them oven and cook the other side (about 4 minutes).

Turn burner down to medium-low and make 6 wells in potatoes. Crack eggs and pour into wells.

Place lid over pan to cook eggs until they are your desired doneness, being careful not to burn potatoes.

Top with cheddar cheese.

Cinnamon Rolls

Dough Ingredients:

3 ¾ cups all-purpose flour

6 tablespoons unsalted butter, cubed

1 package active dry yeast

1 large egg, lightly beaten

½ cup sour cream

½ cup whole milk

⅓ cup sugar

2 teaspoons kosher salt

Non-stick cooking spray

Other Ingredients:

1½ cups confectioners' sugar

4 ounces of cream cheese, softened

¾ cup light brown sugar, firmly packed

½ cup + 4 tablespoons unsalted butter, softened and divided

4 tablespoons whole milk

2 tablespoons ground cinnamon

½ teaspoon vanilla extract

Crisco or oil

Dough Preparation:

In a stand mixer with paddle attachment, combine flour and yeast.

In a saucepan over medium heat, combine milk, sour cream, butter, sugar, and salt. Stir occasionally until mixture is combined, about 3 minutes.

Add milk mixture to flour mixture and mix on low speed. Add egg and mix until dough forms.

Switch paddle attachment to dough hook and mix on medium speed for about 5 minutes.

Spray a large bowl with non-stick spray and place dough in bowl. Turn dough to coat.

Cover bowl and place in a warm place for about an hour and a half or until dough has doubled in size.

Cinnamon Roll Preparation:

Grease iron skillet with Crisco or oil.

On a lightly floured surface, punch down dough and roll out into a 10" by 14" rectangle.

Evenly spread ½ cup of butter on dough.

In a bowl, combine sugar and cinnamon. Sprinkle over top of dough.

Roll dough into one long log, starting with a long side. Pinch to seal along seam.

Slice log into 9 rolls and place in skillet. Cover skillet and place in a warm place for about 45 minutes.

Preheat oven to 350 degrees.

Bake for 30 minutes or until top is golden brown.

Remove from oven and let rest for 30 minutes in skillet on a wire rack.

In a bowl, mix 4 tablespoons butter and cream cheese with a hand mixer until smooth. Add confectioners' sugar, milk, and vanilla. Mix until smooth. Spread over cinnamon rolls.

French Toast with Ricotta & Berries

Dough Ingredients:

4 cups flour (more as needed for dusting surface)

4 eggs, beaten, room temperature

¾ cup warm water

¾ cup butter, melted

¼ cup honey

2 teaspoons salt

1½ teaspoons dry active yeast

Other Ingredients:

1-2 cups raspberries and/or blueberries

1 cup whole milk ricotta cheese

3 eggs

¼ cup honey or maple syrup

Crisco or oil

Garnishes: powdered sugar and maple syrup

Dough Preparation:

In a bowl, mix the eggs, butter, water, honey, salt, and yeast.

Add flour and stir with wooden spoon to combine.

Cover bowl with a towel or plastic wrap and place in a warm place for about 2 hours.

Split dough in half and place one half in freezer for another time.

Use flour to dust surface, rolling pin and hands. Roll out dough and cut into bite-sized pieces. If dough is too sticky, add more flour or put in fridge to chill for 20 minutes. For bite-sized pieces, I find it easiest to roll dough flat, roll it up into a log, and then cut with scissors.

French Toast Preparation:

Preheat oven to 350 degrees.

Grease cast iron skillet with Crisco or oil.

In a bowl, whisk to combine eggs, ricotta and honey. Add dough pieces and berries to mixture. Gently fold with spatula to combine.

Pour mixture into skillet and bake for about 30 minutes or until top is golden brown.

Let stand for 5 minutes. Lightly dust with powdered sugar and serve with maple syrup.

Hash Brown Quiche

Ingredients:

15 ounces of frozen hash browns, shredded

8 ounces of baby portobello mushrooms, diced

1½ cups milk

1½ cups cheddar cheese

1 zucchini, coarsely shredded

3 tablespoons olive oil, divided

3 eggs

½ cup bacon bits

Crisco or oil

Salt and pepper to taste

Preparation:

Preheat oven to 425 degrees.

Grease skillet with Crisco or oil.

In a bowl, combine hash browns, olive oil and salt & pepper to taste.

Pour mix into skillet and press firmly down. Create a "pie crust" with hash browns by packing tightly on the bottom and up the sides of the pan.

Place in oven and bake for about 25 minutes.

In another pan, add 2 tablespoons of olive oil, zucchini and mushrooms. Cook over medium-high heat for about 5 minutes. Drain liquid.

When hash browns are done cooking, remove from oven and turn oven down to 350 degrees. Add half of cheese on top of hash browns. Then add bacon, zucchini and mushrooms, spreading evenly. Top with remaining half of cheese.

In a bowl, whisk eggs and milk together. Salt and pepper to taste and whisk until frothy.

Pour egg mix over top of skillet contents.

Bake for 45 minutes.

Let rest for 10 minutes.

Spinach & Feta Frittata

Ingredients:

1 pound of baby spinach

4 ounces of feta cheese

8 eggs

sea salt and pepper

2 tablespoons olive oil

dried oregano

Crisco or oil

Preparation

Preheat oven to 350 degrees.

Grease cast iron skillet with Crisco or oil.

In a different skillet, heat olive oil over medium-high heat and cook spinach until wilted. Drain spinach and place in cast iron skillet.

In a bowl, beat eggs until frothy. Salt & pepper to taste. Pour over spinach in skillet.

Crumble feta evenly over eggs.

Bake for about 30 minutes or until eggs are done.

Let cool for 10 minutes and season with dried oregano.

Sweet Potato Hash

Ingredients:

1 sweet potato, cubed

1 large egg

¼ red bell pepper, diced

¼ small onion, diced

½ teaspoon chili powder

½ teaspoon cumin

¼ teaspoon garlic powder

salt & pepper

2 tsp olive oil

3-4 tablespoons mozzarella cheese, shredded

2 tablespoons cilantro, chopped

Preparation:

Pierce sweet potato all over with fork and cook on high in microwave until tender, 4-5 minutes per side. Let cool and then dice.

In cast iron skillet, heat olive oil over medium heat and cook onions and red pepper for about 3 minutes or until soft.

Place diced sweet potato in skillet with herbs. Salt and pepper to taste. Cook until potato gets crispy on sides.

Spread sweet potato & onion mix evenly on bottom of pan. Crack egg onto center of mix. Cover and cook until egg is desired doneness.

Top with cheese and place under broiler until bubbly.

Let rest 5 minutes and garnish with chopped cilantro.

Sausage, Egg & Cheese Grits

Ingredients:

1 (8 ounce) package frozen chopped spinach

16 ounces hot Italian sausage or breakfast sausage

2 cups low-sodium chicken broth

3 large eggs, lightly beaten

1 cup gouda cheese, grated

1 cup sharp cheddar cheese, grated & divided

1 cup old-fashioned grits (not instant)

1 cup half and half

2-3 tablespoons green onion, chopped & divided

1½ tablespoons plain cornmeal

½ teaspoon salt

¼ teaspoon ground black pepper

¼ tsp garlic powder

Crisco or olive oil

Optional: red pepper flakes, freshly chopped green onion or parsley, Sriracha or other hot sauce, chopped bacon

Preparation:

Preheat oven to 350 degrees.

Thaw spinach in microwave on defrost (or overnight in fridge) and squeeze out excess liquid.

In a small saucepan, bring broth to a boil. Add grits, salt, and half & half. Stir and reduce heat to simmer. Cook for 12-15 minutes, stirring occasionally until thickened. Remove from heat when done.

In a cast iron skillet, brown sausage over medium-high heat. When sausage is fully cooked, remove from pan and drain. Set both aside.

Add gouda, garlic powder, pepper, green onion and 3/4 cup cheddar cheese to grits and stir until melted.

Add sausage to grits and fold in eggs gently until combined.

Grease cast iron skillet with Crisco or oil and sprinkle cornmeal on bottom and sides.

Place grits & eggs mixture into skillet and spread evenly. Top with remaining cheddar cheese and sprinkle with red pepper flakes, if desired.

Bake for 55 minutes or until golden brown on top and eggs are set.

Remove from oven and set skillet on a wire rack to cool for 30 minutes.

Garnish with green onion and parsley. Serve with hot sauce.

Loaded Baked Potato Breakfast Skillet

Ingredients:

4 eggs

1 medium Idaho potato

6 slices of bacon, cooked & chopped

½ cup whole milk

½ cup cheddar cheese, shredded

2 tablespoons chopped green onion

1 tablespoon vegetable oil

1 tablespoon sour cream

salt & fresh cracked pepper

Garnishes: chopped green onion, sour cream, chopped bacon

Preparation:

Preheat the oven to 350 degrees.

In a bowl, whisk together eggs, milk and sour cream. Add salt & pepper to taste. Set aside.

Dice potato into cubes.

Heat a cast iron skillet over medium heat. Add vegetable oil and coat pan.

Place potatoes in pan and cook until golden brown and tender. Salt & pepper to taste.

Remove from heat and spread potatoes evenly on bottom of pan.

Add chopped bacon and green onions to top of potatoes in an even layer. Pour egg mixture over top.

Bake in oven for 15 minutes or until eggs are set. Touch center to test for doneness.

Garnish with chopped green onion, bacon and sour cream.

Biscuits and Gravy

Ingredients:

1 pound of breakfast sausage

1 can refrigerated biscuit dough

3 cups milk

4 tablespoons all-purpose flour

4 tablespoons unsalted butter

2 teaspoons fresh ground black pepper

Optional: chopped fresh parsley

Preparation:

Preheat oven to 450 degrees.

In a cast iron skillet, cook sausage over medium-high heat until golden brown. Remove sausage from skillet using a slotted spoon and place in bowl.

In a different bowl, mix together flour cheese, baking powder, sugar and salt. Combine with a fork and add milk until it comes together. Set aside.

To heated skillet, add butter and melt. Sprinkle flour

over pan and whisk together to create a paste. Cook mixture for 2 minutes until golden, whisking occasionally.

Add milk to skillet and whisk to combine while scraping browned sausage pieces off bottom of pan to add flavor. Bring mixture to a simmer, about 3 minutes.

Add sausage back into skillet and stir to combine. Crack fresh black pepper to taste and remove from heat.

Place biscuits evenly in skillet on top of mixture.

Bake for about 10 minutes or until lightly browned.

Remove from oven and let rest 5 minutes. Garnish with chopped parsley, if desired.

Appetizers

Skillet Black Bean Queso Dip

Ingredients:

1 (15 ounce) can refried black beans

8 ounces of pepper jack cheese, grated + extra for topping

8 ounces of cream cheese

1 ounce of mozzarella, grated

¾ cup tomatillo salsa verde

¼ teaspoon cayenne pepper

¼ teaspoon red pepper flakes

¼ teaspoon dried parsley

⅛ teaspoon salt

tortilla chips and veggies

Preparation:

Preheat oven to 350 degrees.

Remove pepper jack & cream cheese from fridge to soften.

Make sure your cast iron skillet is well seasoned!

In your cast iron skillet, combine beans and salsa over medium heat, stirring frequently.

Add in cream cheese, cayenne and salt. Stir to combine.

When cheese has melted, add in pepper jack cheese and mix well.

Remove from heat and top with extra pepper jack, mozzarella, parsley and red pepper flakes.

Bake for 15 minutes at 350 degrees.

Remove from oven and place rack in top position in oven. Place skillet on rack and broil until cheese is golden and bubbly, about 2 minutes.

Skillet White Chicken Chili Dip

Ingredients:

1 (14.5 ounce) can white beans, drained

1¼ cups mozzarella/cheddar cheese combination, divided

1 cup cooked chicken, shredded

½ cup sweet corn (fresh or frozen)

⅓ cup diced red peppers

⅓ cup + 1 tablespoon salsa verde

⅓ cup sour cream

2 cloves of garlic, roughly chopped

2 tablespoons cilantro, minced

juice of a half lime

½ teaspoon ground cumin

¼ teaspoon salt

½ tablespoon olive oil

Preparation:

Place oven rack in top position and preheat to 375 degrees.

Oil your cast iron skillet by brushing olive oil on bottom and halfway up sides.

Measure ¼ cup of white beans and set aside.

In a food processor, combine remaining beans, sour cream, garlic, lime juice and cumin. Mix until smooth. Add salt to taste.

Add in chicken, corn, cilantro and a ½ cup of cheese and stir.

Using a spatula, spread mixture evenly on bottom of skillet. Evenly add remaining ¼ cup white beans, red peppers and salsa verde to the top. Add remaining cheese for the top layer.

Bake for 20 minutes or until golden and bubbly.

Skillet Bread and Artichoke Dip

Ingredients:

1 can refrigerated biscuit dough

5 ounces frozen spinach, thawed, pressed & drained

4 ounces of cream cheese, room temperature

⅔ cup marinated artichoke hearts, drained and coarsely

½ cup sour cream

¼ cup mozzarella, shredded + more for topping

¼ cup parmesan cheese, grated + more for topping

¼ cup mayonnaise

1 clove garlic, minced

½ teaspoon Sriracha sauce (or any hot sauce)

Salt and freshly cracked pepper

Crisco or oil

butter, melted

Preparation:

Preheat oven to 375 degrees.

In a bowl, add drained spinach, artichokes, cream cheese, mayonnaise, garlic, hot sauce, parmesan and mozzarella. Mix well. Salt & pepper to taste.

Remove dough from can and cut into 16 equal pieces. Roll each piece into a ball.

Grease your skillet with Crisco or oil.

Place dough balls around edge of skillet, pressing in place to make them all fit and creating a well in the middle of the pan. Brush dough with melted butter.

Spread spinach and cheese mixture evenly into center of skillet so that it touches dough balls. Add parmesan and mozzarella to top of spinach mix.

Bake for 30 minutes.

Remove from oven and move rack to top position. Turn broiler on high.

Add some mozzarella to top of rolls and place under broiler for 2-3 minutes until cheese is golden.

Remove from oven and let rest 10 minutes.

Ultimate Nachos

Ingredients:

1 (15 ounce) can black beans, drained and rinsed

1 pound of ground beef

1 green bell pepper, finely chopped

1 medium tomato, chopped

½ medium yellow onion, finely chopped

2 cups sharp cheddar cheese, shredded

1 packet taco seasoning

1 bag tortilla chips

Optional toppings: olives, avocado, yellow onion, jalapenos, tomatoes, etc.

Garnishes: green onions, salsa, and sour cream

Preparation:

Preheat oven to 350 degrees.

In a separate skillet (not the cast iron), cook beef over medium heat until browned. Add in onion and bell pepper. Cook until onions are translucent and peppers are tender. Drain and add taco seasoning, mixing well.

In a greased cast iron skillet, arrange tortilla chips evenly.

Add half of meat mixture evenly to top of chips. Add half of black beans evenly to top of meat. Add half of cheddar cheese evenly on top of bean layer.

Make another layer of chips and repeat step 4.

Add any optional toppings of choice.

Bake for 10 minutes.

Add garnishes and serve immediately.

Corn and Cotija Cheese Dip

Ingredients:

3 cups fresh corn kernels (or you can use frozen)

1 cup grated cotija cheese + more for topping

4 ounces of cream cheese, room temperature

½ cup sour cream

2 tablespoons olive oil, divided

1 shallot, chopped

1 clove garlic, minced

Salt and fresh cracked pepper

Crackers, bread, tortilla chips or veggies for dipping

Preparation:

Preheat oven to 375 degrees.

Heat a cast iron skillet over medium heat and add 1 tablespoon of oil, garlic and shallot. Stir constantly making sure not to burn.

Add corn and stir. Salt and pepper to taste. Continue

cooking for 5 minutes and remove from heat.

In a bowl, stir to combine cream cheese, sour cream and cotija. Add corn and mix well.

Grease cast iron skillet with 1 tablespoon of oil.

Spread dip evenly over bottom of skillet.

Bake for 12 minutes.

Let rest 5 minutes before serving.

7 Layer Dip

Beef Layer Ingredients:

½ pound ground beef

½ medium yellow onion, diced

2 tablespoons sour cream

1 tablespoon vegetable oil

1 tablespoon tomato paste

1 large garlic clove

½ teaspoon chili powder

¼ teaspoon paprika

½ teaspoon cumin

Salt & pepper

Other Layer Ingredients:

1½ cups shredded Mexican cheese mix

½ cup canned black beans, drained

½ cup canned corn, drained

2 tablespoons fresh cilantro, minced

2 jalapeno peppers, seeded and diced

1 tomato, seeded and diced

½ teaspoon Cumin

½ teaspoon chili powder

salt & pepper

Preparation:

Preheat oven to 350 degrees.

In a cast iron skillet, heat oil over medium heat and add onion. Cook until transparent.

Add beef and cook until nearly done (still some pink). Add garlic, salt & pepper, paprika, cumin, and chili powder. Mix well and continue cooking until beef is no longer pink. Do not overcook.

Add sour cream and tomato paste and stir to combine.

Remove from heat and spread beef evenly on bottom of pan.

Add one layer each of: jalapenos, beans, corn, and then tomatoes.

Season with salt & pepper and cumin. Add cilantro.

Add cheese evenly over top. Season cheese with some chili powder.

Bake for 20 minutes.

Let rest for 5 minutes and serve with tortilla chips.

Entrees

Egg Roll Skillet

Ingredients:

1 pound of ground beef or pork

3 medium carrots, peeled with a potato peeler & then sliced to make thin short strands

1 medium onion, chopped finely

1 small head of cabbage, shredded

1 tablespoon olive oil

5 garlic cloves, minced

3 tablespoons sesame oil

2 tablespoons of fresh grated ginger

2-3 tablespoons soy sauce

2 tablespoons rice vinegar

Optional garnishes: green onions, hot mustard, soy sauce, sweet & sour sauce

Preparation:

In a cast iron skillet, add oil and cook meat and onion over medium heat until onion is translucent and meat is browned.

Turn heat to medium-high and add carrots and cabbage. Cook for 5 minutes, stirring frequently.

In a small bowl, add garlic, ginger, sesame oil, soy sauce, & rice vinegar and mix well.

Pour into skillet and stir to coat meat & cabbage mixture. Reduce heat to medium-low and cook an additional 10 minutes, stirring frequently.

Remove from heat and serve with optional garnishes.

Pizza Tortellini Skillet

Ingredients:

1½ pounds cheese-stuffed tortellini

20 slices of pepperoni

2 cups mozzarella cheese

2 cups marinara sauce

½ cup sliced mushrooms

½ cup water

¼ cup sliced black olives

fresh basil leaves

olive oil

Preparation:

Preheat the oven to 425 degrees.

Grease the inside of a cast iron skillet with olive oil.

Place tortellini in pan and spread evenly. Pour marinara and ½ cup water over tortellini. Do not stir.

Sprinkle cheese over top and place pepperoni evenly.

Add olives, mushrooms and any other toppings of choice.

Bake for 25 minutes.

Remove from oven and let rest for 5 minutes.

Garnish with freshly torn basil leaves.

Chili and Cornbread Skillet

Chili Ingredients:

2 (8 ounce) cans tomato sauce

1 (16 ounce) can kidney beans

1 (15 ounce) can diced tomatoes

1 pound of ground beef

1 cup green bell pepper, chopped

1 cup onion, chopped

½ of a jalapeño, finely chopped

1 tablespoon olive oil

1 tablespoon chili powder

1 tablespoon light brown sugar, packed

2 teaspoons garlic, minced

1½ teaspoons dried oregano

1 teaspoon salt

1 teaspoon cumin

Cornbread Ingredients:

1 cup buttermilk or whole milk, at room temperature

1 cup corn fresh, frozen, or canned

1 cup cornmeal

1 cup all-purpose flour (spoon & leveled)

1 large egg, at room temperature

1 teaspoon baking powder

½ cup unsalted butter, melted and slightly cooled

¼ cup light brown sugar, packed

⅛ teaspoon salt

Preparation:

Preheat oven to 375 degrees.

In a cast iron skillet, heat olive oil over medium heat.

Add beef, onion, peppers, jalapeño, and garlic. Stir occasionally and cook until beef is browned and onions are translucent.

Add the remaining chili ingredients and reduce heat to medium-low. Cover and simmer for 15 minutes, stirring occasionally.

In a bowl, whisk cornbread ingredients until combined.

Remove chili from heat and spread cornbread batter evenly on top.

Bake for 30 minutes.

Remove from oven and let stand 5-10 minutes before serving.

Chicken Pot Pie

Ingredients:

1 refrigerated pie crust (I use Pillsbury)

3 cups cooked chicken, diced

1½ cups frozen peas, carrots & corn

1⅓ cups chicken broth

1 cup half and half

1 egg, lightly beaten

4 tablespoons butter

½ medium onion, diced

1 celery stalk, diced

½ teaspoon salt

½ cup all-purpose flour

¼ teaspoon dried thyme

¼ teaspoon pepper

¼ teaspoon poultry seasoning

Preparation:

Preheat oven to 400 degrees.

In a cast iron skillet over medium heat, melt butter. Add celery and onion and cook for 5 minutes, stirring occasionally.

Add flour and continue cooking for 1 minute. Make sure flour is mixed into butter (no dry flour).

Slowly add chicken broth and whisk into butter & flour mixture. Whisk in half & half until incorporated.

Add poultry seasoning, salt & pepper and thyme. Stir and let simmer for 3 minutes.

Add frozen vegetables and chicken and mix. Remove from heat.

Unfold pie dough and place over top of skillet, tucking under any excess dough.

Brush top of dough with egg. Cut small slits in top of dough to release steam.

Bake 30-35 minutes until crust is golden brown.

Remove from oven and let rest at least 15 minutes before serving.

Lasagna Skillet

Ingredients:

1 (28 ounce) can crushed tomatoes

1 (8 ounce) can tomato sauce

8 whole lasagna noodles, broken into thirds

¾ pound ground beef

¼ pound ground Italian sausage

4 ounces of fresh mozzarella, sliced thin and torn

½ heaping cup of ricotta

¼ cup water

1 tablespoon olive oil

1 medium yellow onion, diced

4 large garlic cloves, minced

½ teaspoon kosher salt

¼ teaspoon crushed red pepper flakes

¼ teaspoon coarse black pepper

Garnishes: freshly torn basil leaves and shaved parmesan

Preparation:

In a cast iron skillet, heat olive oil over medium heat. Add onion and cook until translucent. Add garlic, kosher salt, black pepper and red pepper flakes. Stir and cook for 1 minute.

Add ground beef and Italian sausage and cook until browned, stirring occasionally.

In a bowl, mix tomato sauce, crushed tomatoes and water together.

Layer noodles on top of beef & sausage mixture and pour in tomato & water mixture. Bring to a simmer and reduce heat to medium-low.

Let noodles simmer in sauce, stirring occasionally until tender.

When noodles are al dente, drop ricotta spoonfuls into pan. Stir to slightly break-up ricotta but not completely.

Add mozzarella to top and cover with lid to melt, about 5 minutes.

Remove from heat and garnish with basil and parmesan.

Cheesesteak Skillet

Ingredients:

1 pound of rib eye steak, thinly sliced

4 slices provolone

1 cup baby portobello mushrooms, chopped

1 large onion, halved and then sliced into long strips

2 bell peppers, any color, cut into strips

2 tablespoons soy sauce

1 tablespoon olive oil

1 tablespoon Worcestershire sauce

1 tablespoon lemon juice

1 tablespoon dried basil

½ tablespoon minced garlic

1 teaspoon salt

1 teaspoon black pepper

Optional: hoagie rolls

Preparation:

In a cast iron skillet, heat olive oil for 1 minute over medium heat. Add beef and cook just until it turns brown.

Add soy sauce, Worcestershire sauce, basil, lemon juice, garlic, and salt & pepper and mix well. Add bell peppers, onions and mushrooms and cook for 10 minutes, stirring occasionally.

Add cheese and cover until melted.

Remove from heat and serve as-is or on hoagie rolls.

Chicken Pad Thai

Ingredients:

1 pound boneless & skinless chicken breasts, cut into small strip pieces

8 ounces of rice noodles

1 cup fresh bean sprouts

4½ teaspoons rice vinegar

3 tablespoons vegetable oil

3 tablespoons fish sauce

2 tablespoons fresh lime juice

2 tablespoons packed dark brown sugar

1 tablespoon Sriracha

6 garlic cloves, minced

1 egg, lightly beaten

¼ cup salted peanuts, chopped

½ cup scallions, sliced

½ teaspoon freshly zested lime peel

2 tablespoons fresh cilantro, chopped

Preparation:

In a large bowl, add noodles and pour in hot water to cover. Let stand 10-15 minutes (they should still be a little firm). Drain and press dry with paper towels. Set aside.

In a small bowl, mix together peanuts and lime peel. Set aside.

In a different bowl, combine brown sugar, rice vinegar, fish sauce, lime juice, and chili sauce. Whisk until combined.

In a cast iron skillet over medium heat, heat 1 tablespoon of oil. Add chicken and cook until done. Add garlic and stir. Cook for 1 minute. Transfer chicken to a bowl and set aside.

Pour egg into skillet and cook for 30 seconds without stirring. Flip egg with spatula and cook for an additional 30 seconds until set. Chop with spatula, remove from pan and set aside.

Over medium-high heat, heat 2 tablespoons of oil. Add noodles & bean sprouts. Cook for 2 minutes, stirring frequently.

Add chicken and sauce mixture to pan and cook for 1-2 minutes, stirring frequently.

Remove from heat and garnish with egg, peanuts, scallions, and fresh cilantro.

Skillet Meatloaf

Ingredients:

2 pounds ground beef

1 (14.5 ounce) can diced tomatoes, drained

1½ cups bread crumbs

2 eggs

1 tablespoon olive oil

¼ cup tomato paste

2 tablespoons water

1 medium onion, finely chopped

1 rib of celery, finely chopped

1 carrot, finely chopped

1 teaspoon dried thyme

salt & pepper

Crisco or olive oil

Sauce Ingredients:

½ cup ketchup

2 tablespoons honey

1 teaspoon cumin

Preparation:

Preheat oven to 325 degrees.

Grease a cast iron skillet with Crisco or oil. Set aside.

In a different skillet, heat olive oil over medium heat. Add celery, onion and carrot. Season with a little salt and cook until onion is translucent and carrots & celery are soft. Add thyme and cook 30 seconds. Add tomato paste and water. Stir to combine. Remove from heat.

In a large bowl, beat eggs with a whisk. Add ground beef, tomatoes and bread crumbs. Season well with salt & pepper. Mix with hands until just combined. Add vegetable mixture and mix with hands again until incorporated. Do not squeeze but gently work it with hands.

Place mixture into cast iron skillet and gently press to fit.

Bake for 10 minutes.

While meatloaf is baking, in a small bowl, mix together

sauce ingredients. Spread sauce over top of meatloaf.

Bake for an additional 1-1 ½ hours or until the center reaches 160 degrees. Use a meat thermometer to check temperature.

Stuffed Crust Deep Dish Pizza

Ingredients:

1 premade pizza dough

1 (14 ounce) jar of pizza sauce

2 cups mozzarella cheese, shredded

1 cup sharp cheddar cheese, shredded

6 mozzarella string cheese sticks

all-purpose flour

1 tablespoon olive oil

pepperoni, salami, ham or cooked meat of choice

green bell peppers

fresh tomatoes, seeded and diced

dried basil

dried oregano

garlic powder

garlic butter

Preparation:

Preheat the oven to 450 degrees.

Grease cast iron skillet with olive oil, making sure to get bottom and sides well seasoned.

Prepare a flat surface to roll out the dough. Sprinkle flour on surface and rolling pin to prevent sticking. Roll dough out into large circle.

Transfer dough to pan, draping loosely over sides. Gently press the dough into the pan.

Cut string cheese sticks into 3 pieces each. Roll up cheese into crust (spaced evenly) so crust now fits into pan.

Cover bottom of crust with pepperoni and/or other cooked meats of choice. Add a layer of bell peppers and tomatoes. Add half of mozzarella and half of cheddar cheese. Season with dried basil and garlic powder.

Pour pizza sauce over cheese, spreading evenly. Use a spatula, if needed. Add rest of cheese and season with oregano.

Cook on stove top over medium-high heat to get pan hot, about 3 minutes.

Bake for 10-15 minutes or until crust and cheese are golden brown.

Remove from oven and brush crust with melted garlic butter.

Let stand at least 10 minutes before slicing.

Chicken Enchilada Skillet

Ingredients:

1 pound of chicken, cooked and shredded (use rotisserie to save time)

1 (10 ounce) can red enchilada sauce

3 cups Mexican blend shredded cheese, divided

3 burrito sized soft flour tortillas

1 cup tomatoes, seeded & diced

1 packet taco seasoning

¼ cup fresh cilantro, chopped

¼ cup crumbled cotija cheese

Garnishes: sour cream and avocado

Preparation:

Preheat oven to 350 degrees.

In a skillet (not the cast iron), heat oil over medium-high heat. Add chicken, 3/4 can enchilada sauce, and taco seasoning. Stir to combine. Reduce heat to low and simmer for 2-3 minutes. Add cilantro and stir. Remove from heat and set aside.

In a well-seasoned cast iron skillet, lay 1 tortilla flat on the bottom. Add a layer of chicken and spread evenly. Sprinkle with one cup of cheese.

Make another layer with 1 tortilla, remaining chicken and one cup of cheese.

Make another layer with 1 tortilla, remaining enchilada sauce and one cup of cheese.

Bake for 20 minutes.

Remove from oven and garnish with cilantro, tomatoes, and cotija cheese.

Let rest for at least 5 minutes before serving. Serve with sour cream and avocado.

Deconstructed Stuffed Cabbage

Ingredients:

1 pound of ground beef

3 cups coarsely shredded cabbage

2½ cups water

1 cup brown rice

1 cup mushrooms, sliced

1 medium onion, chopped

2 tubs Knorr concentrated beef stock

1 teaspoon garlic powder

½ teaspoon pepper

Garnish: sour cream

Preparation:

Heat a cast iron skillet over medium-high heat. Cook ground beef, onion, and mushrooms until meat is browned and onion is translucent.

Add stock and water and bring to a boil. Stir in rice,

garlic powder and pepper. Stir in shredded cabbage and mix well. Reduce heat to a simmer and cover. Cook for 35-45 minutes. Check occasionally as you may need to add more water for rice to fully cook.

When rice is cooked and liquid is absorbed, remove from heat.

Serve with sour cream.

Filet Mignon with Garlic & Herb Butter

Ingredients:

4 (10 ounce) thick beef tenderloin filets

2 tablespoons butter

2 tablespoons extra virgin olive oil

salt and pepper to taste

Garlic Butter Ingredients:

½ stick butter, softened

1 tablespoon fresh thyme, chopped

1 tablespoon fresh rosemary, chopped

½ tablespoon garlic, minced

Garlic Butter Preparation:

In a small bowl, mix softened butter and herbs until combined.

Place butter mixture onto a small sheet of aluminum foil. Shape to resemble a stick of butter. Refrigerate and remove about 5 minutes before serving.

Steak Preparation:

Remove beef from refrigerator 30 minutes before cooking to bring to room temperature.

Preheat oven to 425 degrees.

Season beef on all sides liberally with salt & pepper.

In a cast iron skillet, heat olive oil and butter over medium-high heat until hot and bubbly. Your pan must be HOT for the next step.

Place beef filets in pan, giving them space and being sure not to overcrowd them. Do not touch and let them sear for 2 minutes. Flip them over and sear untouched for another 2 minutes.

Place skillet in oven and bake for approximately 5 minutes. See cooking chart below for temperatures.

Remove from oven, transfer to a plate and let rest for 5 minutes.

Top filets with a slice of garlic butter and serve.

Temperatures for beef doneness:

Rare: 130°F to 135°F

Medium Rare: 140°F to 145°F

Medium: 155°F to 160°F

Well Done: 165°F to 170°F

Barbecue Chicken Quinoa Skillet

Ingredients:

2 cups cooked chicken breast, diced or shredded

1 cup uncooked quinoa (if not pre-washed, rinse & drain first)

1½ cups low-sodium chicken broth

1 cup sharp cheddar cheese, shredded

1 cup Monterey jack cheese, shredded

¾ cup sweet corn (frozen, canned or fresh)

½ medium red onion, finely chopped

kosher salt & fresh ground pepper

3 cloves garlic, minced

1 cup grape tomatoes, halved (or a 15 ounce can of diced tomatoes, drained)

½ cup barbecue sauce

3 tablespoons panko breadcrumbs

1 tablespoon extra-virgin olive oil

Garnishes: freshly chopped cilantro, green onions, diced tomatoes, avocado

Preparation:

Preheat oven to 375 degrees.

In a small saucepan, combine quinoa and chicken broth. Bring to a boil. Lower heat, reduce to a simmer and cover. Cook for 14 minutes or until broth is absorbed. Remove from heat and set aside for 5 minutes. Fluff with fork.

In a cast iron skillet, heat olive oil over medium-high heat. Add corn and red onion. Season to taste with salt and pepper. Cook for 2-3 minutes or until onions are translucent.

Add tomatoes and garlic. Cook for 2 minutes, stirring occasionally until tomatoes are soft. Remove from heat.

Add chicken, quinoa, barbecue sauce, and ½ cup of each cheese. Mix well.

Sprinkle remaining cheese evenly on top and then breadcrumbs.

Bake for 25 minutes.

Remove from oven and let rest 5 minutes.

Garnish with freshly chopped cilantro, green onions, diced tomatoes, and avocado, if desired.

Baked Macaroni and Cheese

Ingredients:

1½ cups elbow macaroni or shells

2 cups of sharp cheddar cheese, shredded

2 cups whole milk

3 tablespoons all-purpose flour

3 tablespoons butter or margarine

1 tablespoon Dijon mustard

salt & pepper

Preparation:

Preheat oven to 350 degrees.

In a medium saucepan, bring a pot of salted water to a boil. Cook macaroni so that it's al dente and firm. Do not overcook. Drain well and set aside.

In a well-seasoned cast iron skillet, melt butter over medium heat. Add flour and whisk until it is browned, about 1-2 minutes. Slowly whisk in milk, removing any lumps. Add Dijon and stir. Salt & pepper to taste.

Over medium-high heat, cook until sauce begins to thicken, about 5-7 minutes. Add cheese and whisk until melted and smooth. Remove from heat.

Add pasta to cheese sauce and stir.

Bake for 45 minutes.

Remove from oven and let rest for at least 10 minutes before serving.

French Onion Chicken Skillet

Ingredients:

2 skinless, boneless chicken breast, cut in half lengthwise to create 4 thinner cutlets

3 white onions, quartered and sliced thinly

1¼ cup gruyere cheese, grated

¼ cup white wine

½ cup beef stock

3 tablespoons unsalted butter, divided

9 tablespoons olive oil

2 cloves garlic, minced

1 teaspoon onion powder

1 teaspoon Herbes de Provence

½ teaspoon paprika

¼ teaspoon black pepper

¼ teaspoon garlic onion

¾ teaspoon salt

2 teaspoons fresh thyme leaves, divided use

Preparation:

Place chicken cutlets in a medium bowl and add 2 tablespoons of olive oil. Toss to coat. Add Herbes de Provence, onion powder, salt, black pepper and toss to coat again. Refrigerate and marinate for at least 20 minutes or up to 24 hours.

In a cast iron skillet, heat 3 tablespoons of olive oil over medium to medium-high heat. Place chicken cutlets flat in pan and sear until golden brown, about 3 minutes per side. Remove from pan, place on a plate and cover with foil or lid.

Turn heat down to medium and add 4 tablespoons of olive oil and 2 tablespoons of butter to skillet. Heat until melted and bubbly. Add onions and salt & pepper to taste. Cook until the onions caramelize, about 30-35 minutes, stirring occasionally. You may need to turn the heat down as once they begin to caramelize, they will burn more easily. Cook until they are rich golden brown in color.

Add wine to skillet and cook for 1-2 minutes. Add beef stock and cook for an additional 3-4 minutes. Add garlic, 1 teaspoon thyme and 1 tablespoon butter. When butter is melted, remove from heat.

Return chicken to pan and spoon some of the onion

sauce over the cutlets. Top chicken with cheese.

Place rack in top position in oven and broil skillet until cheese is golden and bubbly, about 3-5 minutes.

Remove skillet from oven. Garnish with remaining thyme leaves.

Apple Butter Pork Chops

Ingredients:

2 pork chop filets

1 (28 ounce) jar apple butter, divided

2 apples, cored and sliced

⅓ cup heavy cream

3 tablespoons butter, divided

2 tablespoons brown sugar, packed

1 teaspoon chili powder

salt and pepper

Preparation:

Season pork chops on both sides with salt & pepper.

In a cast iron skillet, melt 2 tablespoons of butter over medium-high heat. Place pork chops in pan and sear for 3 minutes per side. Place pork chops on plate and set aside.

Melt 1 tablespoon in same skillet over medium-high heat. Add sliced apples and cook for 5 minutes or until softened. Stir in ¾ jar of apple butter, chili powder and brown sugar. Add cream and mix well. Bring to a simmer and reduce heat.

Push apples to sides of pan. Return pork chops to skillet so that they touch the bottom of the pan. Spoon sauce over pork. Cook an additional 4 minutes per side, basting pork with sauce as they cook. When pork is cooked to desired doneness, remove from heat.

Garnish with remaining ¼ jar of apple butter and serve.

Four Cheese Baked Rigatoni

Ingredients:

1 pound of mini rigatoni pasta

8 ounces of fontina cheese, grated

8 ounces of sharp cheddar cheese, grated

8 ounces of gruyere cheese, grated

2 cups milk

⅓ cup mascarpone cheese

⅓ cup panko bread crumbs

¼ cup flour

5 tablespoons unsalted butter

1 shallot, sliced

2 garlic cloves, minced

½ teaspoon olive oil

¼ teaspoon salt

½ teaspoon pepper

¼ teaspoon nutmeg

Preparation:

Preheat your oven to 375 degrees.

Grate the different cheeses and combine them in a large bowl.

Prepare the pasta according to package instructions, cooking for 4 minutes less than the recommended cook time.

Place a large cast iron skillet over medium heat and add the butter and olive oil, once it becomes hot. Sauté the shallots for about 2-3 minutes and sprinkle with a pinch of salt. Stir in the garlic and cook for 30 seconds.

Sprinkle the flour over the shallots and garlic and stir, increasingly to create a roux. Cook for 2-3 minutes until it turns golden then stir in the milk and cook for another 2 minutes.

Add almost all of the grated cheese mixture, reserving half a cup, and the mascarpone. Stir frequently until you get a thick mixture for 3-4 minutes. Season with nutmeg, pepper and salt and toss in the pasta, stirring until evenly coated.

Top with the reserved cheese and bread crumbs. Transfer to the oven and bake for 30-35 minutes or until bubbly and the top starts browning. Serve hot.

Honey Garlic Butter Salmon

Ingredients:

4 salmon fillets

4 tablespoons honey

4 tablespoons butter

2 cloves of garlic, minced

juice from ½ of a lemon

sea salt

Garnish: lemon wedges

Preparation:

Set your oven to broil on medium-high heat.

Add the butter to a cast iron skillet over medium heat until it starts browning and bubbling with a nutty aroma. Stir in the honey, garlic and lemon juice and cook for 30 seconds or until the garlic becomes fragrant. Tur off the heat and pour out half of the butter liquid and set it aside to be used later.

Turn on the heat and toss the salmon steaks in the skillet with the skin side facing down and cook until golden for about 3-4 minutes.

Flip the steaks and transfer the skillet to the oven and broil for 6 minutes.

Season the steaks with salt if desired and drizzle with the reserved melted butter. Serve with a salad or over rice with steamed veggies.

Spicy Shrimp and Quinoa Casserole

Ingredients:

2½ cups cooked quinoa

¾ pound large shrimp, peeled and deveined

1 cup shredded fontina cheese

½ cup sweet onion, chopped

4 medium tomatoes, cut into chunks

1 jalapeno, seeded and chopped

2 cloves of garlic, minced

1 tablespoon tomato paste

3 tablespoons olive oil

2½ teaspoon Cajun seasoning

salt and pepper

Garnish: fresh cilantro, chopped

Preparation:

Preheat your oven to 350 degrees.

Sprinkle the shrimp with a teaspoon of Cajun seasoning and toss well until evenly coated.

Combine the tomatoes with a teaspoon of Cajun seasoning and a tablespoon of olive oil.

Pour 1 tablespoon of olive oil in a cast iron skillet over medium heat and cook the shrimp for 2-3 minutes per side or until opaque then transfer to a platter.

Add the remaining olive oil to the skillet and sauté the garlic, onion and jalapeno until soft. Add in the tomato paste, quinoa, tomato chunks and 1½ teaspoons of Cajun seasoning.

Place the shrimp on top and sprinkle with the cheese. Transfer to the oven and bake for 15 minutes. Turn on the broiler and set it on high for the last 2 minutes of cook time.

Remove from oven and garnish with cilantro. Serve hot.

Creamy Roasted Red Pepper Chicken

Ingredients:

4 boneless skinless chicken breasts

1 (12 ounce) jar roasted red peppers, finely diced

1¼ cup chicken broth

4 ounces of cream cheese

¼ cup diced onion

1 tablespoon butter

2 garlic cloves, minced

½ teaspoon crushed red pepper

¼ cup chopped basil leaves

Preparation:

Melt the butter in a large skillet over medium heat. Sear the breasts for 5 minutes on each side then transfer to a plate.

Sauté the onions in the same skillet and add the garlic after 2 minutes. Stir in the red peppers and continue cooking for a minute or two.

Stir in the cream cheese, broth and crushed red pepper. Lower the heat and simmer.

Stir in the breasts and add the basil. Cook for 2 minutes and serve.

Chicken and Bacon with Mustard

Ingredients:

4 boneless skinless chicken breasts (or 6 thighs)

6 sliced thick cut bacon, diced

1 cup dry white wine (such as Sauvignon Blanc)

¾ cup Dijon mustard, divided

3 tablespoons heavy cream

1 tablespoon whole grain mustard

½ teaspoon smoked paprika

6 sprigs fresh thyme

salt and pepper

Preparation:

Combine ½ cup of Dijon mustard with pepper, paprika and salt in a bowl.

Generously coat the chicken with this mixture and place the coated chicken in zip lock bags and refrigerate for at least 2 hours. For the best results, let it marinate longer.

When ready to cook, remove the chicken from the fridge and set aside.

Place a large cast iron skillet over medium to high heat and add the bacon, stirring until it gets crisp. Transfer to a plate lined with a paper towel.

Brown the chicken in the bacon grease for 4 to 5 minutes on each side. You don't have to wait for the chicken to be done all through. Transfer the chicken and bacon bits to a plate and set aside.

Deglaze the pan with the wine and scrape the browned bits using a wooden spoon. Stir in the whole grain mustard, remaining Dijon and heavy cream, then add the chicken and bacon bits. Stir well and sprinkle with thyme.

Lower the heat and simmer for 15 to 20 minutes until the chicken is cooked through and the sauce is thick.

Serve hot.

Southwest Chicken Alfredo Skillet

Ingredients:

2 boneless skinless chicken breasts, cut into 1 inch cubes

8 ounces of penne pasta

1 cup low sodium chicken broth

1½ cups heavy cream

½ cup parmesan cheese, grated

2 tablespoons olive oil

2 teaspoons minced garlic

1 packet taco seasoning

½ a can black beans, drained and rinsed

½ a can corn, drained and rinsed

½ a can diced tomatoes, drained

salt and pepper

Garnish: Italian parsley or cilantro, chopped

Preparation:

Add oil to a large skillet over medium heat and add in the chicken pieces, browning them for 1 to 2 minutes on each side.

Stir in the minced garlic and cook for an additional minute then stir in the cream, taco seasoning, broth, pepper and salt.

Stir in the pasta and boil lightly, stirring now and then.

Lower the heat and stir in the tomatoes, corn and beans. Cover and cook on low for 20 minutes or until the pasta is cooked al dente.

Stir in the parmesan and sprinkle with fresh parsley or cilantro right before serving.

Skillet Steak

Ingredients:

4 beef tenderloin filets (8-10 ounces each), cut 2 ½ inches thick

1½ cups baby portobello mushrooms, quartered

1½ cups white button mushrooms, quartered

1¼ cups beef broth

1 cup shiitake mushrooms, quartered

¼ cup dry red wine

1 tablespoon all-purpose flour

1 tablespoon butter

1 tablespoon vegetable oil

1 teaspoon kosher salt, divided

¾ teaspoon ground black pepper, divided

1 clove garlic, minced

2 teaspoons tomato paste

1 teaspoon fresh thyme, chopped

Preparation:

Remove the filets fridge the fried at least half an hour before cook time and pat dry with a clean kitchen towel or paper towels.

Preheat your oven to 375 degrees.

Heat oil in a large cast iron skillet over medium heat.

Season the steaks with ½ a teaspoon of pepper and ¾ teaspoon of salt. Brown the steaks in the hot oil for 2-3 minutes then flip the steaks over. Turn off the heat and transfer the skillet to the oven.

Bake the steaks until they reach an internal temperature of 125 degrees, for about 12 to 15 minutes, if you like medium-rare. Cook longer if you prefer your steaks more well done.

Transfer the steaks to a platter and loosely cover with foil.

Melt butter in the same skillet and sauté the garlic and mushrooms, for 4 to 5 minutes until soft.

Whisk the flour into the broth and add it to the skillet together with the wine, thyme, tomato paste and remaining pepper and salt. Bring to a gentle boil and lower the heat to low, simmering for 3 to 5 minutes until thick. Add in the steaks and cook until heated through.

Shepherd's Pie

Ingredients:

2 pounds ground beef

4 russet potatoes, peeled and cubed

12 ounces frozen mixed vegetables

1 cup cheddar cheese, shredded

¼ cup parmesan cheese, shredded

½ yellow onion, diced

1 teaspoon garlic, minced

2 beef bouillon cubes

2 tablespoons Worcestershire sauce

2 teaspoons tomato paste

2 tablespoons butter

1 cup milk

1 tablespoon chives, chopped and divided

black pepper

Preparation:

Boil a pot of salted water over medium to high heat and cook the potatoes until fork tender, for about 20 minutes.

Drain the potatoes and transfer them to a bowl. Add milk and butter and mash to desired consistency. Season with pepper, salt and ½ a tablespoon of chives then set aside.

In a large cast iron skillet placed over medium heat, fry the beef until cooked through, draining off the excess fat and transfer to a bowl.

Sauté the garlic and onions in the same skillet until soft. Stir in the mixed veggies, crumble the bouillon and simmer until the veggies are crisp-tender.

Add in the beef, tomato paste, Worcestershire sauce, pepper and salt, stirring well to combine.

Lower the heat and simmer for 15 minutes then turn off the heat. Use a spatula to compress the layer of beef and top with cheddar cheese. Top with a thick layer of the mashed potatoes and sprinkle with the remaining chives and parmesan.

Bake at 400 degrees until browned for about 20 minutes. Broil on high for 5 minutes for extra browning.

Remove from oven and let stand for 10 minutes before serving.

Broccoli Quinoa Skillet

Ingredients:

1 cup quinoa

1 head broccoli, finely chopped

2 cups milk

1½ cups shredded cheddar cheese, divided

⅓ cup Greek yogurt

⅓ cup Panko bread crumbs

3 boneless skinless chicken breasts, sliced into thin cutlets

2 tablespoons unsalted butter

2 tablespoons olive oil, divided

2 tablespoons all-purpose flour

salt & fresh cracked pepper

Preparation:

Preheat your oven to 350 degrees.

Lightly coat a 9x13 baking dish with non-stick cooking spray.

Cook the quinoa in a large saucepan according to the package directions. Steam the broccoli on top of the quinoa during the last 5 minutes of cook time.

Add a tablespoon of olive oil to a cast iron skillet over medium heat and toast the Panko for about 3 minutes. Transfer to a dish and set aside.

Heat the remaining olive oil in the same skillet, generously sprinkle the pepper and salt on the chicken and brown for 3 to 4 minutes on each side in the skillet. Remove from heat and allow to cool before chopping it.

Add butter to the skillet and place it over medium heat. Stir in the flour and cook for a minute until it turns light brown. Slowly whisk in the milk and cook for 3 to 4 minutes until thick. Stir in the chicken, broccoli, quinoa, Greek yogurt, 1 cup of cheese, pepper and salt.

Spread this mixture into the baking dish and top with the remaining cheese. Bake for about 5 minutes or until the cheese melts.

Serve hot.

Mexican Pasta

Ingredients:

1 pound of ground turkey

1 (15 ounce) can tomato sauce

2 cups uncooked macaroni

2 cups salsa

1½ cups chicken broth

1 cup cheddar cheese, shredded

1 cup corn kernels, frozen, canned or fresh

1 cup canned black beans, drained & rinsed

1 roma tomato, seeded & diced

1 avocado, diced

2 tablespoons cilantro, chopped

1 tablespoon olive oil

Preparation:

Add the olive oil to a saucepan and place over medium heat. Stir in the ground turkey, cooking it until evenly browned for 3 to 5 minutes as you break up the chunks.

Stir in the tomato sauce, pasta, chicken broth and salsa. Bring to a light boil then lower the heat and simmer for about 15 minutes or until the pasta is desired doneness.

Add in the black beans, tomato and corn and stir well to combine. Sprinkle the cheese and stir until it melts, for 2 minutes.

Serve hot with cilantro and avocado.

Deconstructed Stuffed Bell Peppers

Ingredients:

1 pound of ground beef

1 (14.5 ounce) can of whole tomatoes

1 (14 ounce) can of low-sodium chicken broth

1 (8 ounce) can of tomato sauce

1 cup of long grain rice, uncooked

1 cup of Monterey jack cheese, shredded

2 bell peppers, any color

2 tablespoons olive oil

2 cloves garlic

½ of a medium onion

1 teaspoon of soy sauce

salt and pepper

Garnish: chopped green onions

Preparation:

Dice half an onion, 2 bell peppers and 2 cloves garlic. Reserve some of the bell peppers for topping. Sauté the diced veggies in 2 tablespoons of olive oil until soft, then add the ground beef. Season well with pepper and salt.

Once the beef is evenly browned, stir in the tomatoes, soy sauce, tomato sauce and chicken broth. Cover and bring to a boil. Add in the rice, cover and lower the heat to a simmer for 20 to 30 minutes until the rice is perfectly cooked.

After about 20 minutes of cook time, stir the pan so the rice doesn't stick to the bottom. Turn off the heat and sprinkle the cheese on top and cover to allow cheese to melt.

Top with the green onions and the reserved peppers. Enjoy!

Pan-Seared Rib Eye Steak with Garlic Butter

Ingredients:

1 rib eye steak, at least 1½ pounds and cut to at least 1½ inches thick

3 tablespoons butter

2 teaspoons extra-virgin olive oil

2 peeled garlic cloves, whole

3 sprigs fresh parsley

salt & freshly ground black pepper

Optional: Wine, beef stock and butter for deglazing the pan

Preparation:

Season one side of the steak with pepper and salt.

Place a cast iron skillet on medium to high heat until it becomes super-hot. Add the oil, swirling it around to coat the entire surface. Add the steak with the seasoned side facing down and sprinkle the top with salt and pepper and let cook for 2 minutes.

Use a pair of tons to turn the steak then add the butter, parsley and garlic right next to the steak and cook for 2 more minutes as you baste the steak with the melting butter.

Continue with the basting on both sides, flipping the steak every 30 seconds until it's cooked to desired doneness. Turn off the heat and loosely cover the steak, while still in the pan, and let stand for 10 minutes, before slicing it.

Make a pan sauce by deglazing using a splash of wine and letting it simmer for a couple of minutes. Drizzle the sauce over the sliced steak. Enjoy!

Creamy Tomato Basil Pasta

Ingredients:

1 pound of fettuccine

2 cups pasta sauce

1 cup basil pesto

8 ounces of fresh mozzarella cheese, sliced

8 ounces of sheep's milk feta cheese, crumbled

6 ounces of fontina cheese, shredded or diced

2 ounces of cream cheese, softened

1 tablespoon butter

⅓ cup enchilada sauce

½ cup jarred or canned sun-dried tomatoes, drained

½ cup heavy cream

Salt & pepper

Garnishes: fresh basil and grape or cherry tomatoes, halved

Preparation:

Preheat your oven to 350 degrees.

Cook the pasta according to package instructions in a large pot of salted boiling water. Drain pasta once it's cooked and return it to the pot. Add butter, pasta sauce, and chunky basil pesto, sun dried tomatoes, enchilada sauce, cream cheese, sheep's milk feta cheese, heavy cream and fontina cheese. Season well with pepper and salt and toss everything together.

Top the pasta mix with mozzarella and bake for 10-15 minutes. If you wish, you can turn on the broiler and cook for a minute or two until the top browns.

Remove from oven and garnish with fresh basil ribbons. Let stand for 5 minutes before serving with the tomatoes.

Crispy Skin Roasted Chicken

Ingredients:

1 whole chicken

sea salt of kosher salt

olive oil or melted butter

fresh cracked black pepper

Preparation:

Preheat your oven to 375 degrees.

Rinse the chicken and pat it dry using paper towels. Coat it generously with melted butter or olive oil and season with pepper and salt. You can truss the chicken at this point, if desired.

Place a large cast iron skillet over medium to high heat and brown the chicken for 3 minutes on each side.

Transfer the skillet to the oven with the breast side facing up and roast for 1-1½ hours. The juices should run clear and the internal temperature in the thickest part of the chicken thigh should read 165 degrees.

Remove from oven and make a foil tent. Let stand for 20 minutes before carving.

Baked Spaghetti & Meatballs

Ingredients:

18 frozen Italian meatballs

¾ pound spaghetti noodles

1 (24 ounce) jar marinara sauce

2 cups mozzarella cheese, shredded

½ cup parmesan, grated

½ yellow onion, diced

3 cloves garlic, minced

2 tablespoons olive oil

1 teaspoon Italian seasoning

Preparation:

Preheat your oven to 350 degrees.

Add olive oil to a large cast iron skillet over medium to low heat and sauté onions for a minute or two then add the garlic and continue sautéing until fragrant.

Stir in the cooked meatballs, a teaspoon of Italian

seasoning and the marinara sauce. Cover and cook for 20 to 30 minutes.

Meanwhile, cook the spaghetti noodles according to the package instructions but reduce the cook time by 2 minutes.

Use a slotted spoon to scoop out the meatballs and transfer them to a dish. Add the cooked spaghetti to the marinara sauce and about ½ a cup of the drained pasta water. Gently toss until the spaghetti is evenly coated.

Add the meatballs on top and sprinkle with the cheese.

Bake for 20-30 minutes or until the cheese melts fully.

Mexican Polenta

Ingredients:

1 pound of ground beef

1 (16 ounce) tube refrigerated pre-cooked polenta

1 (15 ounce) can black beans, drained and rinsed

1 (14.5 ounce) can diced tomatoes

2 cups Monterey Jack cheese, shredded

1 cup salsa

1 cup corn, frozen, canned or fresh

1 medium yellow onion, diced

2 cloves garlic, minced

½ red bell pepper, seeded and chopped

½ yellow bell pepper, seeded and chopped

½ orange bell pepper, seeded and chopped

3 tablespoons chili powder

2 tablespoons olive oil

1 tablespoons ground cumin

¼ teaspoon cayenne pepper

Garnishes: diced tomato, chopped cilantro, diced avocado, sour cream

Preparation:

Preheat your oven to 375 degrees.

Sauté onion, garlic and bell pepper in oil in a large cast iron skillet over medium heat until soft.

Stir in the turkey, cayenne pepper, chili powder and cumin, breaking up the chunks until it's completely browned.

Add the tomatoes, beans and salsa. Lower the heat and simmer for about 15 minutes. Stir in the corn.

Place the polenta on top and sprinkle with the cheese.

Bake for 20 minutes or until it starts browning and becomes bubbly. Remove from oven and garnish with cilantro and tomatoes. Serve with the additional garnishes, if desired.

Pan Roasted Pork Loin

Ingredients:

1 (3 pound) pork loin

¼ cup low sodium soy sauce

¼ cup olive oil

¼ cup apple cider vinegar

¼ cup Worcestershire sauce

2 tablespoons Italian parsley, chopped

2 teaspoons dry ground mustard

1 tablespoon garlic powder

Preparation:

Preheat your oven to 425 degrees.

Combine all of the ingredients (other than the pork), in a large bowl.

Rinse the pork and pat dry using paper towels then add it to the marinade bowl. Rub in the marinade on all sides and set aside.

Place a cast iron skillet on medium heat until it turns super-hot and sear the marinated meat. Use a pair of tongs to flip the pork every 2 minutes, until perfectly seared.

Place the pan in the oven with the fat side facing up. Roast for half an hour or until cooked to desired doneness. Remove from oven and transfer to a cutting board. Cover loosely with foil and let stand for 10 minutes before serving.

Tuscan Chicken

Ingredients:

2 large boneless skinless chicken breasts, cubed

2 cups Tuscan kale, loosely packed and chopped

8 ounces of cremini mushrooms, sliced

1 cup chicken stock

1 red onion, cut into pieces

½ cup jarred or canned sun-dried tomatoes, drained and rinsed, sliced thinly

¼ cup white wine

1 tablespoon olive oil

1 tablespoon all-purpose flour

¼ teaspoon salt

⅛ teaspoon red pepper flakes

1 sprig of rosemary

salt & pepper

Preparation:

Over medium heat, heat olive oil in a cast iron skillet.

Cook the onion for 2-3 minutes until it is slightly soft. Add mushrooms and cook an additional 3 minutes.

Transfer mushrooms and onions to a bowl. Add ¼ teaspoon salt and 1 tablespoon of flour. Toss to coat.

In your cast iron skillet, add additional oil if needed. Place chicken in pan and season with pepper, salt and red pepper. Cook for 5-7 minutes or until chicken is done.

Add wine and rosemary to pan and cook for 1 minute. Pour in stock, sun-dried tomatoes and the onion-mushroom mix. Cook for 3-4 minutes, stirring frequently until sauce thickens.

Stir kale into pan until it wilts.

Serve hot with farro or rustic bread.

Seafood Paella

Paella Ingredients:

12 ounces of medium shrimp, deveined, cooked & peeled

4 cleaned small squid, chopped

1 (15 ounce) can tomato sauce

3 cups chicken stock, plus more if needed

1 cup dry white wine

2 cups medium-grain Spanish paella rice or risotto rice

3 tablespoons extra virgin olive oil, divided

1 onion, finely chopped

3 garlic cloves, minced

½ cup cherry tomatoes, cut in half

½ cup cooked spicy sausage, chopped

3 teaspoons smoked paprika

pinch of saffron threads

kosher salt and pepper

Garnish: Italian parsley, finely chopped

Mussels Ingredients:

12 mussels, scrubbed and de-bearded

1 cup chicken stock

½ cup water

3 cloves garlic, minced

2 shallots, minced

1 tablespoon extra-virgin olive oil

1 tablespoon butter

Preparation:

For the paella:

Heat 2 tablespoons of olive oil in a large cast iron skillet over medium to high heat. Sauté the onions for 3-4 minutes until soft. Add the garlic and sauté for about a minute until fragrant.

Stir in the tomato sauce and season with pepper, then add the saffron and paprika. Cook for 4-5 minutes, then add the squid. Cook for 1 minute before adding the rice. Stir well.

In a separate pan, boil the wine and chicken stock and pour the mixture over the rice. Increase the heat and add salt, if needed.

Lower the heat to low and simmer for 15-20 minutes. Add more tomato sauce, if needed.

For the mussels:

Add butter and olive oil to a large cast iron skillet over medium heat. Once the butter has melted, sauté the minced garlic and shallots until tender, for 1-2 minutes.

Pour in the water and stock, then add the mussels. Cover and cook for 5 minutes, after which they should all have opened. Cook for 2 more minutes, if some are yet to open. Stir the mussels so they are covered by the sauce and discard any that haven't opened.

Once the rice is ready, arrange the tomatoes, shrimp and sausage and cook for 8-10 minutes. Flip the shrimp and let cook for a few more minutes.

Arrange the mussels on the paella and drizzle with the remaining olive oil. Sprinkle with parsley and serve hot.

Beef and Broccoli

Ingredients:

1 (1 pound) flank steak, trimmed and sliced thin

5 cups broccoli florets

1 cup onion, sliced into wedges

½ cup beef broth

½ cup soy sauce

3 tablespoons cornstarch, divided

2 tablespoons brown sugar

1 teaspoon ground ginger

½ teaspoon red pepper flakes

2 tablespoons cold water

1 tablespoon garlic, minced

3 tablespoons olive oil, divided

Preparation:

Combine the brown sugar, beef broth, soy sauce, pepper flakes, 1 tablespoon of cornstarch and ginger in a bowl, then set aside.

In a different bowl, combine garlic, 2 tablespoons of cornstarch and water. Add the beef and mix well, until evenly coated.

Add 2 tablespoons of oil to a skillet over medium to high heat and brown the beef for 3 to 4 minutes. Transfer to a plate and set aside.

Sauté the onions and broccoli in the same pan until soft for about 5 minutes.

Add the cooked beef and stir well, then pour in the broth mixture and cook until thick, for about 5 minutes.

Serve over a bed of rice.

Chicken Cacciatore

Ingredients:

8 chicken thighs (or 4 breasts)

1 (14.5 ounce) can fire roasted diced tomatoes

1 (8 ounce) can tomato sauce

8 ounces of cremini mushrooms, sliced

1 green bell pepper, sliced

1 red bell pepper, sliced

1 large Vidalia onion, diced

¼ cup red wine

1 tablespoon olive oil

3 cloves of garlic, minced

1 tablespoon Italian seasoning

kosher salt and fresh ground pepper

Garnishes: chopped Italian parsley and basil

Preparation:

Preheat your oven to 425 degrees.

Add olive oil to a large cast iron skillet and place over medium heat. Generously rub the chicken with pepper and salt, then place it in the skillet with the skin side facing down. Cook until the skin is crisp and golden, then turn it and cook it on the other side for about 5 minutes. Transfer the chicken pieces to a plate and drain the excess fat.

Sauté the onions until soft in the same pan and add in the peppers. Cook until they start to get soft, for about 2 minutes. Add in the mushrooms and cook for about 2 minutes, until they start getting soft. Stir in the garlic and cook until fragrant, then add the wine and Italian seasoning. Continue cooking until the wine reduces by half.

Next add the tomato sauce and tomatoes and lower the heat to a gentle simmer. Season with pepper and salt and add the browned chicken – with the skinless side facing down.

Turn off the heat and place the skillet in the oven and roast for about half an hour until the chicken is ready.

Garnish with fresh parsley and basil and serve hot.

Ham & Penne Skillet

Ingredients:

3 cups ham, cubed

16 ounces of penne noodles, uncooked

3 cups chicken broth

2 cups frozen peas, thawed

2 cups milk

½ cup parmesan cheese, grated

½ cup yellow onion, chopped

¼ cup all-purpose flour

3 cloves of garlic, minced

1 tablespoon olive oil

½ teaspoon dried parsley

½ teaspoon dried basil

¼ teaspoon dried oregano

¼ teaspoon red pepper flakes

¼ teaspoon pepper

Preparation:

Add a tablespoon of olive oil to a large cast iron skillet over medium heat then add the onions and ham. Cook until the onions become soft. Stir in the garlic, oregano, parsley, pepper flakes and the pepper and cook for about 2 minutes.

Add in the milk, broth, penne noodles and flour and cook for 10 minutes.

Stir in the peas and cook until the pasta cooks through, for about 5 minutes.

Sprinkle the parmesan on top and cook until it melts. Serve hot.

Salisbury Steak with Mushroom Gravy

Steak Ingredients:

1 pound of ground beef

¼ cup panko bread crumbs

2 tablespoons tomato paste

1 teaspoon dry ground mustard

1 teaspoon Worcestershire sauce

½ teaspoon onion powder

salt & pepper

Gravy Ingredients:

3 cups beef stock

4 ounces of white mushrooms, sliced

1 large Vidalia onion, diced

2½ tablespoons all-purpose flour

1 tablespoon butter

1 teaspoon fresh thyme leaves, chopped

½ teaspoon garlic powder

1 teaspoon Worcestershire sauce

kosher salt and pepper

Garnish: chopped Italian parsley or chives

Preparation:

Use your hands to combine the beef, Worcestershire sauce, bread crumbs, mustard, tomato paste, pepper, onion powder and salt. Divide the mixture into 4 and make each portion into a ½-inch patty.

Add 1 teaspoon of olive oil into a cast iron pan and cook the patties until evenly browned for about 3 minutes on each side then transfer to a plate. Drain off the excess fat.

Sauté onions in the skillet until soft then stir in the mushrooms and cook until they are soft. Add the flour, thyme and garlic powder and cook until well incorporated, for 1 minute.

Add the stock and scrape the browned bits off the bottom of the skillet. Add in the Worcestershire sauce and bring to a boil. Lower the heat once the sauce starts thickening and add in the butter. Season with pepper and salt if desired.

Add the beef patties to the gravy and cook until heated through. Turn off the heat and garnish with chives and parsley. Serve hot.

Corned Beef and Cabbage

Ingredients:

1 (3 pound) corned beef brisket

1 head savoy or green cabbage, cored and sliced

3 cups water

1 (12 ounce) bottle of premium beer

1 Vidalia onion, sliced

3 carrots, roughly chopped

3 celery stalks, roughly chopped

1 teaspoon dry ground mustard

½ teaspoon dried thyme

½ teaspoon mustard seeds

1 bay leaf

1 tablespoon canola oil

1 tablespoon olive oil

1 tablespoon butter

1 teaspoon kosher salt

½ teaspoon fresh ground pepper

Preparation:

Preheat your oven to 300 degrees.

Heat the oil in a large skillet over medium heat and place the brisket with the fat side facing down. Cook for about 5 minutes until brown, then flip it and cook for another 5 minutes. Turn off the heat and drain the excess fat.

Pour the beer over the brisket and add in the carrots, mustard seeds, celery, mustard, bay leaf and water. Cover and put the skillet in the oven, cooking for 3 hours.

When you are left with an hour of cook time, heat olive oil and butter in a large skillet and sauté the onion until soft. Stir in the cabbage and cook until it starts caramelizing. Season with pepper and salt and transfer to the oven and cook for about 15 minutes, until both the cabbage and onions start browning.

Cooked brisket should be soft enough to pull apart using a fork. Remove from oven and cover with foil. Let stand for 10 minutes before serving.

Serve with the caramelized cabbage.

Chicken Tortilla Casserole

Sauce Ingredients:

2 (28 ounce) cans diced tomatoes

1½ cups chicken broth

4 tablespoons olive oil

1 yellow onion, roughly chopped

4 cloves garlic, chopped

3 teaspoons chili powder

2 teaspoons cumin

1½ teaspoons salt

1 teaspoon oregano

Casserole Ingredients:

2 pounds of boneless skinless chicken breasts

15 small corn tortillas

4 cups mozzarella cheese, shredded

2 tablespoons taco seasoning

Garnishes: chopped cilantro and cotija cheese

Preparation:

Preheat your oven to 375 degrees.

Add 2 tablespoons of olive oil to a large skillet and sauté the onions over medium heat. Lower the heat and stir in cumin, chili powder, garlic, oregano and salt. Cook for about 3 minutes until fragrant.

Stir in the chicken broth, tomatoes, and garlic and cook on low heat until the sauce thickens and turns deep red. Transfer the sauce to a blender or food processor and process until smooth then set aside.

Season the chicken breasts on both sides. Add 2 tablespoons of olive oil to a cast iron skillet and brown chicken over medium heat on each side. Pour the sauce on top and simmer for about 10 minutes until the chicken cooks through. Take chicken out and shred it with forks, then set aside.

Dip 5 tortillas in the sauce and arrange them on your cast iron skillet. Add a serving of chicken, some cheese and some sauce. Repeat the layering and finish off with a layer of the tortillas, cheese and sauce.

Cover with foil that has been sprayed with cooking spray (to prevent cheese from sticking) and bake for about 20 minutes until the cheese melts.

Remove from oven and garnish with cotija and cilantro.

Southern Fried Chicken

Ingredients:

1 pound of chicken breasts or wings

2 cups buttermilk

2 eggs

2 teaspoons baking powder

1½ teaspoons baking soda

1 teaspoon paprika

1 teaspoon hot sauce

all-purpose flour

salt and pepper

vegetable oil for frying

Preparation:

Combine all the spices and liquid ingredients in a bowl until well blended. In a separate bowl, mix the baking soda and baking powder. Add to the wet ingredients, whisking until frothy.

Put 2 cups flour in a shallow dish next to the wet mixture.

Dredge the chicken pieces in the flour then dip it into the wet mixture, ensuring it's fully coated. Return to the flour and dredge again and place on a plate.

Heat at least 1 inch of oil in a skillet until it's hot enough to fry the chicken. Fry chicken in batches, so they do not crowd the pan. Fry until golden and transfer to a dish lined with paper towels, then cook the remaining batch. Season with pepper and salt and serve hot.

Skillet Steaks with Herbed Gorgonzola Butter

Ingredients:

4 ribeye steaks

olive oil

kosher or sea salt and fresh ground pepper

Gorgonzola Butter Ingredients:

4 tablespoons Gorgonzola cheese

4 tablespoons butter, softened

1 tablespoon fresh parsley, chopped

Preparation:

Rub both sides of the steaks with pepper and salt and tightly wrap each with plastic wrap. Refrigerate for at least 4 hours or overnight, for the best results.

Remove from the refrigerator 30 minutes before cook time in order to bring up to room temperature.

Place a large cast iron skillet over medium heat until hot, then add some olive oil and swirl it around for even coating.

Cook the steaks for 2 minutes on each side until well browned and cooked to desired doneness.

Turn off the heat and let stand in the skillet for 5 minutes.

Combine the gorgonzola cheese, butter and parsley in a bowl until well creamed and serve a tablespoon of the butter-cheese mixture on each steak.

Serve hot.

Shrimp with Orzo, Feta and Asparagus

Ingredients:

1½ pounds medium shrimp, peeled and deveined

2 cups asparagus, ends trimmed and chopped into 2-inch pieces

1 cup whole wheat orzo

½ cup fresh basil leaves, chopped

½ cup crumbled feta cheese

1½ tablespoons olive or canola oil, plus more for the pasta

2 medium cloves garlic, minced

½ teaspoon red chili flakes

juice from 2 lemons

1 tablespoon extra-virgin olive oil

kosher salt and freshly ground black pepper

Preparation:

Cook the orzo according to package instructions in a skillet filled with two-thirds full with salted water. Drain and toss with canola or vegetable oil, then set aside.

Use a paper towel to wipe the skillet and place it over medium heat. Pour in the oil and sauté the chili flakes and garlic until fragrant, stirring constantly for a minute. Toss in the asparagus and season well with pepper and salt. Cook for about 4 minutes until crisp-tender.

Use a spatula to move the asparagus to one side of the skillet and add in the shrimp. Cook for 4 minutes turning occasionally until the shrimp turn opaque.

Pour the orzo into the skillet and stir in the lemon juice, feta, most of the basil and olive oil. Add pepper and salt, if needed. Turn off heat, garnish with the remaining basil and serve hot.

Beef Enchilada Skillet

Ingredients:

1 pound of ground beef

15 small corn tortillas, cut into wedges

2 cups cheddar cheese, shredded

1 (4 ounce) can sliced black olives, drained

1 (4 ounce) can green chilies, with juice

1 (10 ounce) can enchilada sauce

1 tablespoon olive oil

1 packet taco seasoning

Garnishes: sour cream, sliced avocados and chopped cilantro

Preparation:

Preheat your oven to 350 degrees.

Add olive oil to a large cast iron skillet over medium heat and brown the beef for about 10 minutes, breaking up all the chunks. Add in the green chilies, taco seasoning mix and half the olives. Cook for 1 minute, then add the enchilada sauce and ½ a cup of cheese. Turn down the heat and simmer for 5 minutes. Add in the tortillas and cover with sauce, cooking until they absorb most of it for a minute or so.

Sprinkle with the shredded cheese and place in oven to bake for about 10-15 minutes, until melted. Remove from oven and top with avocado, sour cream, cilantro and remaining olives.

Serve hot.

Creamy Chicken and Mushrooms

Ingredients:

4 boneless skinless chicken breasts

8 ounces of baby portobello mushrooms, sliced

1 teaspoon lemon juice

4 tablespoons butter

1 tablespoon shallots, minced

salt & pepper

Sauce Ingredients:

1½ cups heavy cream

¼ cup port wine or dry white vermouth

¼ cup chicken stock

2 tablespoons fresh parsley, chopped

salt and pepper

Preparation:

Preheat your oven to 400 degrees.

Rub the chicken breasts with lemon juice and season with pepper and salt.

Add butter to a cast iron skillet over medium heat and cook until it stars bubbling. Sauté the green onions or shallots until soft but not brown. Add the mushrooms and sauté without browning. Sprinkle with salt.

Roll the breasts in the butter mix in the skillet.

Bake for 10 minutes then flip the breasts and continue baking for 8 minutes.

Remove from oven and transfer the chicken to a warm plate but leave the mushrooms in the skillet.

Add the wine and stock to the mushrooms and boil over high heat until it looks syrupy. Stir in heavy cream and simmer over low heat. Add a few drops of lemon juice and stir in the broccoli and cook until crisp tender.

Pour the mushroom sauce over the chicken. Sprinkle with parsley and serve.

Barbecue Ranch Chicken & Cheese Skillet

Ingredients:

4 boneless skinless chicken breasts

1 (15 ounce) can of black beans, drained and rinsed

1 (15 ounce) can of corn, drained and rinsed

1½ cups long grain white rice (not instant)

1½ cups water

1 cup chicken broth

1 tablespoon olive oil

½ cup Mexican shredded cheese

¼ cup barbecue sauce

¼ cup fresh cilantro, chopped

¼ cup cilantro lime ranch dressing (or regular ranch dressing)

salt and pepper

2 roma tomatoes, seeded & diced

Garnishes: chopped cilantro, green onion, and avocado

Preparation:

Preheat your oven to 350 degrees.

Add oil to a deep cast iron skillet over medium heat. Rub the chicken with pepper and salt on each side, then add it to the skillet with the skin side facing down. Cook for 5 minutes per side, adding barbeque sauce to each side, then transfer to a plate.

Stir in the beans and corn to the skillet and cook until heated through, for about 2 minutes. Stir in the ranch and cilantro until well combined.

Toss in the rice until evenly coated and pour in the water, broth, pepper and salt. Return the chicken to the skillet without stirring.

Cover and bake in the oven for 30 minutes.

Top with the tomatoes and cheese and bake for another 5 minutes or so until the cheese melts.

To serve, top with avocado, green onions and cilantro.

Chicken Parmesan Pasta

Ingredients:

3 boneless skinless chicken breasts, cubed

1 (24 ounce) jar marinara sauce

16 ounces of rigatoni pasta

½ cup parmesan cheese, grated

½ cup mozzarella cheese, shredded

2 tablespoons Italian dressing

salt and pepper

Garnish: chopped fresh basil

Preparation:

Add the chicken and Italian seasoning to a large cast iron skillet and sprinkle with pepper and salt. Over medium heat, cook until it browns, for about 5 minutes.

Add in the whole jar of marinara, box of pasta, plus the water and bring to a quick boil. Cover and lower the heat to a simmer for 15 minutes, or until the pasta is done.

Top with parmesan and mozzarella and cook until

melted, for about 2 minutes or set the skillet in the oven and broil for 4 minutes. Serve with fresh basil.

Chicken Sausage with Potatoes & Sauerkraut

Ingredients:

12 ounces cooked chicken sausage (4 links), halved lengthwise and sliced

3 medium Yukon Gold potatoes, halved and thinly sliced

1 medium onion, thinly sliced

1½ cups dry white wine

1½ cups sauerkraut, rinsed

1 tablespoon extra-virgin olive oil

½ teaspoon freshly ground pepper

¼ teaspoon caraway seeds

1 bay leaf

Preparation:

Add oil to a cast iron skillet over medium heat and sauté the onion and sausage until it starts browning, about 4 minutes. Add the sauerkraut, potatoes, caraway seeds, wine, beef and pepper and bring to a gentle simmer.

Cook covered for about 15 minutes until the potatoes are soft and the liquid has reduced. Remove the bay leaf and serve hot.

Macadamia Crusted Mahi Mahi

Ingredients:

2 (6 ounce) Mahi Mahi fillets

1 egg

¼ cup panko bread crumbs

¼ cup macadamia nuts, finely chopped

2 tablespoons unsweetened coconut milk

olive oil

salt and pepper

Preparation:

Preheat your oven to 450 degrees.

Add the macadamia nuts to a food processor and process until crumbly. Mix the crumbled nuts with the panko and set aside.

Whisk the milk and egg in a bowl and set aside.

Season both sides of the fish with pepper and salt.

Cover the base of a cast iron skillet with olive oil and

place over medium heat. Dip the mahi mahi in the milk mixture and dredge in the nut mix.

Cook in the hot oil for 3 minutes per side and transfer the skillet to the oven, baking for 10 minutes or until firm to the touch.

Serve hot.

Bacon, Mushroom & Thyme Chicken

Ingredients:

4 chicken thighs (or breasts)

1 tablespoon olive oil

2 teaspoons Italian seasoning

salt and pepper

Sauce Ingredients:

8 ounces of white mushrooms, sliced

1 cup heavy cream

6 slices bacon, cooked and chopped

1 tablespoon fresh thyme leaves

1 tablespoon olive oil

1 teaspoon garlic powder

½ teaspoon salt

¼ teaspoon pepper

Preparation:

Preheat your oven to 350 degrees.

Place a large skillet over medium heat until hot, then add the chicken and Italian seasoning. Sprinkle with pepper and salt and sear for about 2 minutes on each side, until browned. Transfer the skillet to the oven and bake for about 20 minutes or until the chicken is cooked through. Remove from oven and transfer the chicken to a plate.

Pour olive oil in the skillet and cook the mushrooms until soft. Stir in the heavy cream, garlic powder, bacon, thyme, pepper and salt. Simmer until the sauce thickens, then toss in the chicken and cook for a minute until heated through. Serve hot.

Chicken Parmesan

Ingredients:

2 boneless skinless chicken breasts, sliced in half lengthwise and lightly pounded

1½ cups marinara sauce

¾ cup mozzarella cheese, shredded

½ cup parmesan cheese, grated

3 tablespoons olive oil

1 teaspoon fresh thyme, chopped

1 teaspoon fresh rosemary, chopped

1 teaspoon fresh Italian parsley, chopped

2 tablespoons unsalted butter, cut into small pieces

salt and pepper

Preparation:

Preheat your oven to 500 degrees.

Combine 3 tablespoons of olive with the fresh herbs and some pepper and salt to taste.

Rub each side of the chicken with the herb mixture and set aside for a few minutes.

Place a large cast iron skillet over high heat and cook the chicken for about 3 minutes, until well browned. Turn off the heat and pour the tomato sauce over the chicken.

Sprinkle the breasts with mozzarella and parmesan and top with the butter pieces.

Place the skillet in the oven and bake the chicken until cooked through and the cheese melts, for about 5 minutes.

Remove from oven and serve hot.

Pork Chops in Mushroom Gravy

Ingredients:

6 bone-in or boneless pork chops

1 pound of cremini mushrooms, sliced

1 cup onion, sliced thin

¾ cup beef stock

¾ cup chicken stock

¼ cup all-purpose flour

2 teaspoons olive oil

salt and pepper

Preparation:

In your cast iron skillet, sear the chops in very hot oil over medium to high heat, then transfer to a warm plate.

Add 1 teaspoon of olive oil to the skillet and sauté the onions and mushrooms for 5 minutes, until they start browning.

Lightly sprinkle with flour and cook until it has all been absorbed.

Add the chicken and beef stock and cook for 2 minutes, scraping the browned bits from the bottom of the pan. Add the chops and cook for 20 minutes uncovered or until the sauce is thick to your liking. Cover and cook for an additional 10 minutes on low heat or until the pork chops are done.

Gnocchi with Spinach and Chicken

Ingredients:

1 pound cooked chicken breast, shredded

1 (17.5 ounce) package potato gnocchi (not frozen)

8 ounces of baby portobello mushrooms, sliced thin

2 cups baby spinach leaves

1½ cups whole milk

1 cup chicken broth

½ cup parmesan cheese, grated

2 tablespoons salted butter

2 tablespoons all-purpose flour

½ teaspoon nutmeg

1 teaspoon onion powder

4 cloves of garlic, minced

kosher salt and freshly ground black pepper

Preparation:

Preheat your oven to 425 degrees with the rack placed in the upper-middle position.

Melt butter in a deep cast iron skillet over medium heat. Whisk in the flour to form a roux for 3 minutes, then stir in the milk and broth until well blended. Simmer, whisking frequently for 5 minutes until thick. Whisk in the garlic powder, nutmeg, pepper, onion powder and salt.

Add in the mushrooms, shredded chicken, spinach and uncooked gnocchi and stir until evenly coated. Top with parmesan and transfer to the oven. Bake for about 15 minutes or until the sauce is bubbly.

Serve hot.

Cajun Chicken & Rice

Ingredients:

4 boneless skinless chicken breasts, pounded thin

2¼ cups low sodium chicken broth

1 cup rice, uncooked

½ green bell pepper, diced

½ red bell pepper, diced

4-5 teaspoons cajun seasoning, divided

Garnish: chopped cilantro

Seasoning Ingredients:

1 teaspoon salt

1 teaspoon garlic powder

1½ teaspoon paprika

½ teaspoon cayenne pepper

½ teaspoon black pepper

½ teaspoon onion salt

½ teaspoon oregano

¼ teaspoon red pepper flakes

Preparation:

Rub both sides of the chicken breast with 2 teaspoons of Cajun seasoning and set aside.

Add olive oil to a cast iron skillet over medium heat and brown the breasts for one minute per side, then transfer to a plate.

Lower the heat and stir in the peppers, rice, broth and remaining Cajun seasoning, stirring well to combine.

Add the chicken on top of the rice, cover and cook on low for about 20 minutes until the chicken is cooked through and the liquid absorbed.

Remove from heat, garnish with cilantro and serve.

Chicken Fried Steak

Ingredients:

2 pounds of cube steak, cut into 6 pieces

25 saltine crackers, crushed

2 eggs

1 cup all-purpose flour, divided

1 teaspoon seasoned salt

¼ teaspoon cayenne pepper

⅓ cup milk

vegetable oil

salt and pepper

Gravy Ingredients:

2 cups whole milk

¼ cup all-purpose flour

Preparation:

Sprinkle the steak with pepper and salt.

Pour ½ cup flour on a plate and set aside.

Combine the Saltine crumbs, remaining flour, cayenne pepper and seasoned salt in a shallow dish.

Whisk ½ cup milk and eggs in a shallow dish. Dredge the steak in flour, then dip in the milk mixture and coat with the Saltine mix.

Heat some oil in a cast iron skillet and cook the coated steak over medium heat. Once cooked, transfer to a plate lined with paper towels.

Spoon or pour the remaining oil into a bowl (heat-proof) and return ¼ cup of oil to the skillet. Add flour to the skillet and whisk to form a roux, for about 1 minute. Whisk in the milk and season with pepper and salt.

Pour over the steak and serve.

Sides

Garlic Parmesan Bread

Ingredients:

1 can buttermilk biscuits

¼ cup parmesan cheese, grated

2 garlic cloves, minced

3 tablespoons butter

2 tsp Italian seasoning

Preparation:

Preheat your oven to 350 degrees.

Melt the butter in a cast iron skillet and stir in the parmesan, garlic and Italian seasoning. Cut the biscuits into quarters and add to the skillet. Turn off the heat and transfer to the oven and bake for about 15 minutes.

Remove from oven and serve hot.

Whole Wheat Bread (Outback Steakhouse Style)

Ingredients:

4 cups whole wheat flour

2 cups warm water

2¼ teaspoons granulated active dry yeast

1½ teaspoons kosher salt

1 tablespoons rolled oats

olive oil

few pinches of coarse salt

Preparation:

Preheat your oven to 400 degrees.

Combine the flour, yeast and salt in a bowl and gently pour in the water. Use a wooden spoon to mix until well combined, to form a sticky dough.

Cover with plastic wrap and a kitchen towel and place the bowl in a warm spot in your kitchen for 1 hour.

Grease the bottom of a cast iron skillet using olive oil

and set aside.

Sprinkle some flour on top of the dough and knead using floured hands. Transfer kneaded dough to the skillet. Use the wooden spoon to spread it around evenly in the pan.

Lightly brush the top of the dough with 2 teaspoons of olive oil. Sprinkle the salt and oats on top and bake for about 35 minutes or until the top forms a deep brown crust.

Loaded Mashed Potatoes

Ingredients:

7 small potatoes

4 slices of bacon, cooked and chopped

1½ tablespoons canola or olive oil, divided

1 teaspoon coarse salt

1½ cups sharp cheddar cheese, shredded

1 tablespoon butter

salt and pepper

Garnishes: sour cream and chopped green onions

Preparation:

Preheat your oven to 425 degrees.

Poke a few holes using a fork into the potatoes and place them on a microwave safe plate. Pop in the microwave and cook for 10 minutes.

Place a tablespoon of oil in a cast iron skillet, brushing some on the sides. Arrange the potatoes and bake for 10 minutes or until soft, then remove from oven.

Smash the potatoes using a potato masher and add butter on each of the smashed potatoes and top with pepper and salt. Brush the sides with oil and bake for 10 more minutes until crisp and golden. Sprinkle the top with cheese and bacon bits and bake until the cheese melts.

Serve with sliced green onions and dollops of sour cream.

Southern Cornbread

Ingredients:

2 cups self-rising cornmeal

1½ cups buttermilk

2 large eggs, lightly beaten

¼ cup bacon drippings or oil

½ teaspoon sugar

½ teaspoon baking soda

¼ teaspoon salt

Preparation:

Preheat your oven to 400 degrees.

Add the oil or bacon drippings to a skillet and pop in the oven to heat up.

Combine all the other ingredients and add to the hot skillet and bake for about 20 minutes, until golden.

Enjoy!

Buttermilk Biscuits

Ingredients:

3 cups all-purpose flour, plus more for surface

1 cup buttermilk

½ cup vegetable shortening, plus more for skillet

¼ cup unsalted butter, melted

2 tablespoons sugar

2½ teaspoons baking powder

½ teaspoon salt

½ teaspoon baking soda

Preparation:

Preheat your oven to 450 degrees.

Mix the flour, baking powder, sugar, salt and baking soda. Use a fork to cut the shortening until it resembles cornmeal.

Gradually stir in the buttermilk until well combined.

Place the dough on a floured surface and knead about 3

times, then roll out to a ½-inch thickness using a rolling pin.

Use a 2-inch cutter to cut the dough into circles.

Arrange the biscuits on a greased cast iron skillet, gently pressing on them. Brush with half the butter and bake for about 15 minutes or until golden. Enjoy!

Country-Fried Corn

Ingredients:

6 ears corn

3 slices of bacon

⅔ cup water

¼ cup milk

1 tablespoon butter

1 tablespoon sugar

2 teaspoons cornstarch

¼ teaspoon black pepper

salt

Optional: pinch red pepper flakes

Preparation:

Carefully use a very sharp knife to remove kernels from ears of corn. Place the kernels in a bowl.

Use the back of a knife to scrape the cobs, then add to the bowl with the kernels.

In a large cast iron skillet, crisp up the bacon, then transfer to a plate lined with a paper towel. Crumble or chop bacon.

Add the corn kernels to the skillet with the bacon fat and cook for a minute over medium heat. Stir in sugar and water and cook for 5 minutes, until thick.

Mix the cornstarch with milk in a small bowl and add it to the skillet, cooking until thick.

Stir in the peppers, butter and salt. Sprinkle with the bacon bits. Serve hot.

Skillet Dinner Rolls

Ingredients:

4½ cups all-purpose flour, sifted

1¼ cups milk

¼ cup unsalted butter

¼ cup warm water

1 large egg

2 packets yeast

1 tablespoon sugar

5 tablespoons sugar

¾ teaspoon salt

1 teaspoon kosher salt

3 tablespoons unsalted butter, melted

non-stick spray

Preparation:

Preheat your oven to 375 degrees.

Combine the sugar and yeast with warm water and set aside.

Heat sugar, butter and salt with milk until just warm and set aside.

Whisk the egg into the yeast mixture and add it to the milk mixture. Stir in the flour and cover with a kitchen towel and let sit for 15 minutes.

Knead the dough using a stand mixer fitted with a dough hook for 5 minutes.

Roll out the dough on a lightly floured surface and divide it into 18-tennis sized balls. Cover and let sit for 25 minutes.

Spray a large skillet with cooking spray and arrange the balls. Sprinkle with kosher salt and bake for about 12 minutes or until the tops turn golden.

Remove from oven and brush with melted butter and serve.

Scalloped Potatoes

Ingredients:

6 medium Yukon Gold potatoes, peeled and thinly sliced

2 cups Gruyere cheese, shredded

1½ cups milk

3 tablespoons all-purpose flour

3 tablespoons unsalted butter

2 cloves garlic, minced

1 sprig thyme

salt and pepper, to taste

Preparation:

Preheat your oven to 400 degrees.

Place a cast iron skillet over medium heat and melt the butter. Stir in the flour to form a roux for 30 seconds. Stir in the thyme, garlic, pepper and salt to taste. Whisk in the milk until you achieve a smooth consistency. Turn off the heat and transfer the mixture to a bowl.

Arrange the potatoes in the skillet in a spiral pattern and

season the layers with pepper and salt. Sprinkle cheese on each layer.

Pour the milk mixture on the potatoes and top with cheese. Cover the skillet with foil and bake for 1 hour.

Remove foil and bake for 10 minutes or until the top turns golden.

Remove from oven and let stand for 5 minutes before serving.

Mexican Potatoes

Ingredients:

3 large skin-on white potatoes, diced

1 pound of ground beef

1½ cups Colby cheese, shredded

1 cup Pico de Gallo

3 tablespoons olive oil

2 tablespoons taco seasoning

1 tablespoon water

Garnish: sour cream

Preparation:

Heat oil in a cast iron skillet over medium heat. Once the oil is shimmering hot, toss in the potatoes. Cook for about 20 minutes, turning occasionally until the potatoes are soft.

Meanwhile, brown the beef in a separate skillet and drain off the excess fat. Stir in water and taco seasoning in the pan and cook for 2 more minutes.

Pour the beef over the cooked potatoes and sprinkle cheese on top.

Place the skillet in oven and broil on high for 3 minutes until the cheese melts.

Remove from oven and serve with sour cream and Pico de Gallo.

Hot German Potato Salad

Ingredients:

2 pounds of gold or red potatoes, thinly sliced

6 strips of thick-cut bacon, cooked and chopped

1½ cups red onion, thinly sliced

½ cup apple cider vinegar

¼ cup of water

3 cloves of garlic, minced

2 stalks celery, thinly sliced

2 tablespoons real maple syrup

1½ tablespoons stone ground mustard

salt & pepper

Garnish: chopped green onions

Preparation:

Cover the potatoes with water in a big stock pot. Season with salt and bring to a rolling boil. Cook until the potatoes are fork tender but not too soft. Drain the water and cover the pot with the potatoes inside.

Meanwhile, brown the bacon in a large cast iron skillet until crisp, then transfer to a plate lined with paper towels. Let it cool, then crumble it.

Add the celery and onion to the skillet with the bacon fat on medium and sauté until soft. Stir in the garlic and cook until fragrant.

To make the sauce, mix maple syrup, apple cider vinegar, water and mustard in a jar and shake it well. Add to the skillet.

Pour the skillet contents into the stock pot and let stand for 10 minutes until most of the sauce gets absorbed. Season with pepper and salt and stir in the bacon bits.

Serve with sliced green onions.

Vegetable Fried Rice

Ingredients:

2 cups of cold, cooked rice (white or brown)

1 cup of broccoli

1 carrot

½ yellow onion

1 tablespoon olive oil

Sauce Ingredients:

2 tablespoons soy sauce

¼ teaspoon toasted sesame oil

¼ teaspoon sugar

pinch of salt

Preparation:

Combine 2 tablespoons of soy sauce, ¼ teaspoon sugar, ¼ teaspoon toasted sesame oil and some salt in a bowl, then set aside.

Steam the broccoli and carrot in a pot for about 5

minutes until crisp-tender.

Heat olive oil in a skillet over medium heat and toss in the onion, broccoli and carrot. Cook for 5 minutes.

Stir in the cold rice and mix well, until heated through. Stir in the sauce and cook for 2 minutes then serve.

Hasselback Potatoes

Ingredients:

8 baby Yukon Gold potatoes

8 tablespoons unsalted butter, melted

4 cloves of garlic, minced

4 tablespoons grated Parmesan

4 tablespoons parsley, rosemary, and thyme, minced

salt and pepper

Preparation:

Preheat your oven to 425 degrees.

Slice a thin layer off each potato lengthwise and set aside.

Place each potato with the flat side down and make slices that don't go all the way through, then gently fan out the slices.

Combine the garlic, melted butter and minced herbs, then set aside.

Brush the bottom of the skillet with the butter mix as well as the potatoes and reserve the remaining mixture.

Gently place the potatoes in the skillet and top with parmesan. Sprinkle with pepper and salt to taste.

Place in the oven and bake for an hour, basting the potatoes with the butter mix every 15 minutes or so until crisp and golden.

Serve hot.

Cheesy Enchilada Rice

Ingredients:

1 cup uncooked rice

1 cup Mexican shredded cheese

1 cup canned black beans, drained and rinsed

1 cup corn kernels, canned, frozen or fresh

2 cloves garlic, minced

1 small onion, diced

1 bell pepper, diced

1 tablespoon olive oil

¾ cup mild enchilada sauce

½ cup mild green enchilada sauce

½ teaspoon chili powder Coupons

¼ teaspoon oregano

¼ teaspoon cumin

2 tablespoons cilantro, chopped

salt & pepper

Preparation:

Cook rice according to the package instruction in a saucepan with 1½ cups of salted water.

Add olive oil to a large skillet over medium heat and sauté the onion, garlic and pepper for 2 minutes until soft, being careful not to burn the garlic.

Stir in the cooked rice, enchilada sauce, black beans, cumin, chili powder and oregano until evenly combined.

Turn off the heat and sprinkle with cheese. Cover to let the cheese melt for 2 minutes. Serve hot with cilantro.

Desserts

Banana Upside Down Cake

Ingredients:

1 cup all-purpose flour

4 medium-sized ripe bananas

¾ cup light brown sugar, tightly packed

¾ cup granulated sugar

¾ cup buttermilk

½ cup unsalted butter

2 teaspoons baking powder

1 large egg

1 tablespoon vanilla extract

pinch of salt

Preparation:

Preheat your oven to 350 degrees.

Melt the butter in a cast iron skillet over medium heat until it starts bubbling. Carefully sprinkle the sugar over the bubbling butter and let it sit for 1 minute without stirring, until it dissolves. Turn off the heat.

Set aside the ripest banana in your bunch that you will use for the cake batter. Peel the remaining bananas and halve them. Cut each half into lengthwise quarters and slowly arrange them on the butter and sugar combo in the shape of a circle.

For the batter: mix flour, baking powder, sugar and salt in a mixing bowl, then set aside.

In a different bowl, mash the banana you had set aside and combine with buttermilk, egg and vanilla. Pour this mixture into the bowl of dry ingredients and stir well to combine, being careful not to overmix. The mixture should resemble pancake batter.

Gently pour the cake batter over the banana pieces in the pan, being careful not to move them out of place.

Place the skillet in your pre-heated oven and bake for 40 minutes or until golden.

Remove from the oven and set aside to cool. Let it stand for about 15 minutes before inverting the cake on the plate.

Serve when cool and store the remaining cake in an airtight container. Eat the cake within 2 days before the bananas oxidize and become brown. Enjoy!

Double Chocolate Chip Cookie

Ingredients:

1¼ cup all-purpose flour

1 cup milk chocolate chips

2 eggs

½ cup unsalted butter, softened

½ cup sugar

½ cup dark chocolate cocoa powder

⅓ cup dark brown sugar, tightly packed

½ teaspoon baking soda

¼ teaspoon salt

1 teaspoon vanilla

Preparation:

Preheat your oven to 350 degrees. Coat a cast iron skillet with cooking spray and set aside.

Combine the flour, baking soda, cocoa and salt in a medium mixing bowl, then set aside.

Beat the butter and two sugars together using an electric mixer set on medium to high speed for about 2 minutes, until light and fluffy. Beat in the eggs, one at a time, on medium to low speed until evenly mixed. Pour in the vanilla.

Add the dry ingredients a little at a time, on medium speed until just combined. Take out the bowl from the mixer and fold in the milk chocolate chips using a rubber spatula until well combined.

Carefully press the dough in the greased skillet and bake for 15 minutes. Though the cookie will look undercooked, it's going to settle and firm up as it cools. Let stand for 10 minutes before serving the cookie.

Drizzle the top with hot fudge and top with a generous dollop of ice cream or whipped cream. Keep the leftovers in an airtight container. Enjoy!

Peach Cobbler

Ingredients:

1 (29 ounce) can of sliced peaches, drained

2 cups milk

2 cups sugar

2 cups flour

2 sticks of butter, melted

2 teaspoons baking powder

Preparation:

Preheat your oven to 350 degrees.

Pour the sliced peaches into a cast iron skillet.

Pour the melted butter evenly over the peaches.

Combine the flour, baking powder, sugar and milk in a mixing bowl to form a batter. Pour mixture over the peaches.

Bake for about 30-45 minutes or until the edges become crispy and the top browns evenly.

Texas "Sheet Cake" Skillet

Ingredients:

2 cups all-purpose flour

2 cups sugar

2 eggs

8 ounces of butter, cubed

1 cup water

½ cup sour cream

4 tablespoons unsweetened cocoa powder

1 teaspoon baking soda

½ teaspoon salt

1 teaspoon vanilla

Frosting Ingredients:

3 ¾ cup powdered sugar

¾ cup pecan bits

4 ounces of butter, cubed

6 tablespoons milk

3 tablespoons unsweetened cocoa powder

Garnish: vanilla ice cream

Preparation:

Preheat your oven to 350 degrees.

Spray a 10-inch cast iron skillet with non-stick cooking spray.

Heat the cocoa, butter and water in a pan over medium heat. Bring to a boil, then turn off heat.

In a large mixing bowl, combine the flour, baking powder, sugar and salt.

Whisk the eggs in a different bowl and pour in vanilla and sour cream and continue whisking. Pour this mixture over the dry ingredients, using a wooden spoon to stir until well combined.

Pour the cocoa-butter mixture over the batter and use a hand mixer or whisk to combine until the batter turns glossy.

Pour the butter into the prepared skillet and bake for about 30 minutes or until an inserted toothpick comes out clean. Remove the cake from the oven and set aside to cool.

Meanwhile, prepare the frosting by combining cocoa, butter and milk in a saucepan over medium heat and bring to a boil. Turn off the heat and mix in the powdered sugar using a hand mixer until glossy. Use a wooden spoon to stir in the pecan bits.

Gently spread the frosting over the now warm cake and let stand for 10 more minutes as it cools. Serve with ice cream.

Peanut Butter Cup Cookie

Ingredients:

1 (30 ounce) tube chocolate chip cookie dough

6 chocolate peanut butter cups

1 cup chocolate chips

Garnish: vanilla ice cream

Preparation:

Preheat your oven to 350 degrees.

Divide the cookie dough into two equal pieces. Press half the cookie dough into a cast iron skillet (bottom and sides) and top with chocolate chips and chocolate peanut butter cups.

Top with the remaining cookie dough and bake for about 20 minutes or until the edges start browning.

Remove from oven and let cool slightly. Serve with ice cream. Enjoy!

Red Velvet Cookie

Ingredients:

1 cup flour

⅔ cup white chocolate chips

½ cup sugar

⅓ cup brown sugar

1 egg

6 tablespoons butter, softened

1½ tablespoons unsweetened cocoa powder

1 tablespoon red food coloring

1 teaspoon vanilla

½ teaspoon baking soda

½ teaspoon salt

Garnishes: vanilla ice cream, chocolate syrup or hot fudge

Preparation:

Preheat your oven to 350 degrees.

Grease a cast iron skillet and set aside.

Combine the sugars with the butter using an electric mixer on high speed until light and fluffy, for about 2 minutes. Add the vanilla and egg and continue mixing until well combined then add the food coloring.

In a separate bowl, whisk the flour, baking soda, cocoa and salt. Add this mixture to the wet ingredients until well combined. Use a rubber spatula to mix in the white chocolate chips, then press the dough into the prepared skillet.

Bake for about 20 minutes until set and remove from oven. Let stand for 10 minutes before serving with your desired toppings. Enjoy!

Apple Crisp

Ingredients:

6 apples, peeled, cored and diced

½ cup light brown sugar, tightly packed

3 tablespoons unsalted butter

1 tablespoon fresh lemon juice

¾ teaspoon cinnamon

1 vanilla bean

pinch of salt

Topping Ingredients:

1½ cup oats

1 cup chopped pecans

½ cup light brown sugar, tightly packed

¼ cup all-purpose flour

½ teaspoon cinnamon

¼ teaspoon salt

¼ teaspoon nutmeg

6 tablespoons cold unsalted butter

Preparation:

Preheat your oven to 350 degrees.

Combine the pecans, brown sugar, oats, cinnamon, flour, salt and nutmeg in a mixing bowl.

Divide the butter into tiny pieces and use your hands to rub the butter pieces into the mixture, until fully combined.

In a large bowl, toss the apple chunks with brown sugar, lemon juice, salt and cinnamon and set aside.

Melt 3 tablespoons of butter in an oven proof skillet over medium heat. Meanwhile, split the vanilla bean and scrape it into the butter, stirring for a minute or so.

Add the apples to the skillet and turn up the heat to medium-high and cook for 5 minutes, stirring frequently.

Turn off the heat and sprinkle streusel over the apple mixture and bake for 30 minutes. Remove from oven and let cool slightly before serving with ice cream. Enjoy!

Bourbon Peach & Blueberry Crumble

Ingredients:

6 cups sliced peaches (roughly 5-6 peaches)

1 cup blueberries

¼ cup sugar (you may need to add more depending on how sweet & tart your fruit is)

¼ cup bourbon

2 tablespoons cornstarch

1 teaspoon fresh lemon juice

1 teaspoon cinnamon

½ teaspoon vanilla extract

¼ teaspoon lemon zest, grated

Topping Ingredients:

1 cup all-purpose flour

1 cup rolled oats

1½ sticks cold unsalted butter, cubed

½ teaspoon salt

½ cup sugar

2 tablespoons heavy cream

Preparation:

Preheat your oven to 375 degrees.

Combine the peaches, bourbon, blueberries, cornstarch, sugar, cinnamon, lemon zest and vanilla in a large mixing bowl until evenly combined.

In a separate bowl, mix the oats, flour and salt for the topping. Add the cold butter chunks in the mixture and use a mixer to combine. (Alternatively, you can toss the ingredients in a food processor until crumbly.) Mix in the heavy cream until the dough holds together.

Spread the filling in a large cast iron skillet and sprinkle the topping over the filling.

Place the skillet on a baking sheet and bake uncovered for about 30-40 minutes, or until the edges turn brown and the fruit bubbles.

Blueberry Cobbler

Blueberry Mix Ingredients:

4 cups fresh blueberries (or frozen blueberries, thawed)

2 tablespoons sugar

2 tablespoons unsalted butter

2 tablespoons water

1 tablespoon lemon juice

2 teaspoons corn starch

1 teaspoon cinnamon

Topping Ingredients:

1¼ cups all-purpose flour

¾ cup whole milk

½ cup sugar

1½ teaspoons baking powder

5 tablespoons butter, cubed

1 teaspoon vanilla extract

½ teaspoon salt

Preparation:

Preheat your oven to 400 degrees.

Melt 2 tablespoons of butter in a cast iron skillet over medium heat and add blueberries. Stir until evenly coated with butter, then stir in the remaining blueberry mix ingredients. Bring to a slow boil, then simmer for about 3 minutes and turn off the heat.

For the topping: mix the flour, salt, baking powder and sugar. Crumble the butter pieces into the flour, then add the vanilla extract and milk. Stir using a large spoon until fully combined.

Use the spoon to drop the topping over the blueberry mix. Bake for about 20 minutes or until the fruit starts bubbling and the topping turns golden.

Remove from oven and set aside to cool. Enjoy!

Black Cherry Cake

Ingredients:

1 ¾ cups all-purpose flour

1 ½ eggs (beat 1 egg and add half)

¾ cup milk

¼ cup brown sugar

5 tablespoons butter

1 ½ teaspoons active dry yeast

¾ teaspoon salt

Topping Ingredients:

2 1/2 cups black cherries, fresh or frozen, pitted

2 tablespoons unsalted butter, melted

2 tablespoons light brown sugar

Glaze Ingredients:

1/2 cup confectioners' sugar

1 tablespoon milk

1/2 teaspoon vanilla extract

Preparation:

Lightly grease a cast iron skillet and set aside.

Warm the milk, butter and brown sugar in a saucepan until all of the butter is almost melted. Turn off the heat and mix in the yeast. Let stand for 10 minutes until frothy.

Combine the flour and salt in a large mixing bowl. Add the yeast mixture and eggs and mix until just combined. Do not overmix. Pour the batter into the greased pan and cover with plastic wrap that is lightly coated with non-stick spray.

Place the pan in a warm spot and let stand for 45 minutes. If you are preparing this the night before, you can place the pan in your fridge for 8 hours or overnight, then bake in the morning.

Preheat your oven to 350 degrees.

Remove the plastic wrap once the dough has risen and spread the cherries on top. Sprinkle with brown sugar and finish off with the melted butter.

Bake for 30 minutes then reduce your oven's temperature to 325 degrees and bake for 10 -15 more minutes (or until the edges start pulling from the skillet and the top browns).

Meanwhile, prepare the glaze by combining all the ingredients and whisking them until smooth. Remove the cake from the oven and let cool slightly. Drizzle with the glaze and enjoy!

Skillet S'mores

Ingredients:

8 large marshmallows

1 cup chocolate chips

graham crackers

Preparation:

Preheat your oven to 450 degrees.

Add chocolate chips to a seasoned cast iron skillet.

Cut marshmallows in half (or use an equivalent amount of small marshmallows) and arrange over the chocolate chips.

Bake for 7-9 minutes or until the marshmallows start browning.

Remove from oven and serve with graham crackers.

Snickerdoodle Biscuits

Biscuit Ingredients:

3½ cups all-purpose flour (use White Lily brand for extra light & fluffy biscuits)

1⅓ cups buttermilk

1 stick butter, cubed and softened

4 tablespoons shortening, cubed

1 tablespoon sugar

1 tablespoon baking powder

½ teaspoon baking soda

¾ teaspoon salt

Topping Ingredients:

¼ cup sugar

1 tablespoon butter, melted

1 teaspoon cinnamon

Preparation:

Preheat your oven to 425 degrees.

Grease a cast iron skillet and set aside.

For biscuits: combine flour, baking soda, baking powder, salt and 1 tablespoon of sugar in a large mixing bowl.

Use your fingers to rub the pieces of butter and shortening into the mixture until it becomes crumbly. Add in the buttermilk and mix until well combined.

Lightly coat a ½-cup measuring cup with non-stick cooking spray and scoop 6 heaps of dough into the greased pan – place the first heap at the center and the others around it.

Combine the cinnamon and ¼ cup of sugar and sprinkle it over the biscuits.

Bake for 20-25 minutes until the tops turn golden. Brush the biscuit tops with melted butter and top with the remaining cinnamon–sugar mixture.

Printed in Great Britain
by Amazon

54741748R00143